The Eucharist,
Gift of Divine Life

The Eucharist,
Gift of Divine Life

**Prepared by
The Theological-Historical Commission
for the Great Jubilee of the Year 2000**

*Translated from the Italian by
Robert R. Barr*

A Crossroad Faith & Formation Book
The Crossroad Publishing Company
New York

The Crossroad Publishing Company
370 Lexington Avenue, New York, NY 10017

Original edition: *Eucarestia, sacramento di vita nuova*
copyright © 1999 by Edizioni San Paolo (Milan)

English translation copyright © 1999 by
The Crossroad Publishing Company

Library of Congress Cataloging-in-Publication Data

Eucarestia, sacramento di vita nuova. English.
   The Eucharist, gift of divine life / prepared by the Theological-Historical Commission for the Great Jubilee of the Year 2000 ; translated from the Italian by Robert R. Barr.
      p.   cm.
   ISBN 0-8245-1806-3 (pbk.)
      1. Lord's Supper – Catholic church. 2. Mass. 3. Catholic Church – Doctrines.   I. Theological-Historical Commission for the Great Jubilee of the Year 2000.   II. Title.
   BX2230.5.E88   1999
   234′.163′08822 – dc21   99-39019

1   2   3   4   5   6   7   8   9   10   04   03   02   01   00   99

Contents

Gift of Divine Life

For twenty centuries, Christians in all places, in various rites, have celebrated the legacy of Jesus to his Apostles the evening of the Last Supper: "Do this in remembrance of me" (Luke 22:19), a practice that engages their whole faith. For twenty centuries, although they celebrate the Eucharist, Christians have never understood it exhaustively. This gift of Jesus is of a wealth that has never been plumbed. It is a mystery with a thousand facets and a multiplicity of names — meal, sacrifice, memorial, Mass, all of these names fitting the gift which Jesus has given us, but none of them exhausting its meaning. Jesus himself did not name what he was giving us. He simply performed the actions and spoke the words. The simplest of actions, the one by which the disciples of Emmaus recognized the Risen One, was the "breaking of the bread" — so called because he himself, in his Gospel, had identified himself with bread: "I am the bread of life that came down from heaven. Whoever eats of this bread will live forever" (John 6:51).

The Pope has asked that the jubilee year be "intensely Eucharistic" (*TMA, no. 55*). The International Eucharistic Congress to be held in Rome June 18–25, 2000, has taken as its central theme of reflection: "Jesus Christ, Only Savior of the World, Bread for a new life."

More than ever, a disenchanted world has need of knowing that Jesus Christ is its only Savior. More than ever, a world ravaged by hunger has need of knowing that the only bread that can satisfy it is a bread that gives a new life. Every Eucharist shows forth the dawn of Easter, that morning all new when the empty tomb became the cradle of a new humanity. The Eucharist is a bread that makes those who receive it hungry — a bread that causes hunger as much as it satisfies it, for it stirs the taste for a new life, God's life in us.

A French philosopher, Gabriel Marcel, has written: "To love

someone is to tell that person: 'You will not die.'" This is what is said to each of us by the One who has conquered death in instituting the Eucharist: "Be glad, rejoice at the heart of the Eucharist. You will not die! Indeed, a new world is spread before you. The Reign of Heaven is at hand: it is already here."

CARDINAL ROGER ETCHEGARAY

Abbreviations

AAS   *Acta apostolicae sedis*

DS   *Enchiridion Symbolorum, Definitionum et Declarationum de Rebus Fidei et Morum,* ed. H. Denzinger and A. Schönmetzer (1965)

PG   J. Migne, *Patrologia graeca*

PL   J. Migne, *Patrologia latina*

TMA   *Tertio Millennio Adveniente,* With the Coming of the Third Millennium, apostolic letter of John Paul II on the Great Jubilee of the Year 2000

Introduction

The Church is about to cross the threshold of the year 2000. It will mark the event by celebrating the gift that it has received from the Savior, the Eucharist. At this most solemn moment of the history of humanity, we can better place ourselves before the person of the "Word made flesh" by having faithful recourse to the words that Christ addressed to his disciples at the Last Supper: "Do this in remembrance of me" (Luke 22:19)

True, two thousand years have not yet passed since these words were pronounced. According to the most reliable calculations, Jesus died on April 7, A.D. 30: thus, the Eucharist would have been instituted on April 6. He had been born more than thirty years before, but here we know neither the day nor the year with certitude.

Still, how are we to celebrate the anniversary of the coming of the Son of God into the world without commemorating, in a special manner, the Eucharist, through which, in a certain sense, his coming into our universe is continually renewed? The best way to place ourselves once more before the person of the "Word made flesh" is precisely to return to the decisive moment in which he who had loved us manifested his limitless love by giving himself to humanity in the Eucharist.

Jesus himself has willed that his memory be perpetuated among us not by way of a simple remembrance, but through a memorial consisting of the celebration of the Eucharist. Thus, he expects from us this Eucharistic homage on the occasion of the Jubilee. The Church, then, is preparing for the Jubilee by meditating on the Eucharist and making an effort to penetrate more deeply into its mystery, an effort to grasp more fully its meaning and value, an effort to live it with greater faith and love.

This will be an appropriate way not only to enter the year 2000, but actually to lay the groundwork for all of the future development of the Church, since, through the Eucharist, Christ "comes" into the world. With his coming, the community founded by him expands in the direction of the unification of all humanity through the sharing of his divine life.

The purpose of the present volume is to contribute to this Eucharistic coming of Christ. Our means of doing so will be to write about the hope that continually grows as human destiny is more and more deeply transformed. The Pope has written in *Tertio Millennio Adveniente* (On the threshold of the third millennium) that the Jubilee will be "intensely Eucharistic." The continuity between the Eucharist and the mystery of the Incarnation is very important. The Eucharist, efficacious sign of the living, operative presence of the Lord in the midst of his Church, prolongs the Incarnation. In the "Bull of Indiction" of the Holy Year, the bull officially proclaiming the Great Jubilee, *Incarnationis Mysterium* (The mystery of the Incarnation), John Paul II is clear:

> For two thousand years, the Eucharist has been the cradle in which Mary has placed Jesus, entrusting him to the adoration and contemplation of all peoples, that, through the humility of the Spouse of Christ, the glory and power of the Eucharist may gleam all the more — that Eucharist that the Church celebrates and preserves at its heart. Under the sign of the consecrated bread and wine, Christ Jesus, risen and glorified, the Light of nations (Luke 2:32), reveals the continuation of his Incarnation. He is still risen and alive in our midst, to nourish believers with his body and blood.
>
> (*Incarnationis Mysterium*, no. 11)

Chapter 1

Value and Importance
of the Eucharist

The Divine Ingenuity

The Eucharist, which plays so important a role in Christian faith, is the most surprising of the divine inventions. It manifests the ingenuity of a wisdom that at the same time is the foolishness of love. We admire the ingenuity of so many human inventions, reflecting as they do such exceptional qualities of intelligence and ability. Divine inventions are on an infinitely higher level, but are intended to penetrate human existence more profoundly. The entire revelation of the work of salvation is of an astonishing nature; and the Eucharist constitutes a pinnacle of mystery, where, in the simplest possible way, the fulfillment of the divine design has far surpassed any possible expectation. The Eucharist secures for humanity, in the order of faith — by way of an ultimate gift that will mark the path of the Church to the end of the world — that which was acquired once and for all by the work of the redemption.

The Eucharist is not simply "one of the sacraments." It surely belongs to the sacramental "economy" and cannot be honored to the detriment of baptism, confirmation, sacramental forgiveness. However, it possesses a unique excellence, as it is the sacrament in which is given not only grace, but the very author of grace. In this way the person of Christ is manifested in the most immediate and real manner.

How could we fail to be surprised at the words "This is my body" and "This is the cup of my blood"? How could we fail to admire the avenue chosen by a sovereign wisdom to offer a presence in flesh and blood that, in our way of thinking, could only have been a remembrance of a past over and gone? Where we can see but bread and wine, we stand before the assertion of

13

this presence. How could we fail to be astonished at the fact that the one who is God offers himself as food and drink to his very creatures? It is such an abasement and condescension on his part that we stand in bewilderment. The one who is Lord places himself entirely at our disposition, at our service. How could we fail to wonder why the one who consummated his sacrifice on the Cross and crowned it with the triumph of his resurrection could have willed that his offering be repeated through all time in the Eucharistic celebration? If the offering of Calvary was sufficient, to overflowing, for obtaining salvation and grace for all human beings, then why must Jesus, why must God, invent a new presence in the Christian assembly?

To all of this astonishment, and to all of these questions, there is but one response: Everything in the Eucharist derives from love carried to extremes. All emerges from a limitless will to give. It is the divine love that, for the succor of human beings and in order to guarantee them the highest destiny, has become unsurpassably inventive in the actions and words of Jesus that have instituted the Eucharist at the Last Supper. Inasmuch as our astonishment is so great, we must make a continual effort toward a better understanding of the intentions of this love.

It is always necessary to delve more deeply into our faith. Here, it is a matter of searching out, in the life and teaching of Jesus as well as in the teaching of the Church, the basic meaning of the Eucharist.

It is also a matter of accepting the validation of doctrine through the experience of the Christian life, the experience of the whole Church and each of its members. The Eucharist plays an essential role in the growth of the Christian community. That community continues to nourish, with the meal of Communion, those called to bear witness to Christ and his good news in the world. The good news imparts strength to those so conscious of their frailty, and joy to those in sorrow. It stimulates, with a spiritual inebriation, in view of an apostolic task, those who could be tempted to close themselves off from that news. And thus the good news shows that the intense divine love it expresses obtains its end, the transformation of human life. The divine ingenuity is fecund.

The Eucharist, Deed of Salvation

Eucharist and Incarnation

The Eucharist enables us to grasp more concretely the meaning and value of the Incarnation. The presence of the body and blood of Christ, proclaimed by the words of consecration and celebrated as the "mystery of faith," refers us to the very reality of the Incarnation, a reality taken on by the Son of God as actual human reality. The deed with which he who was God came down from heaven to become a human being and to lead a human life like our own is reproduced in the Eucharist. When the words "This is my body, . . . This is the cup of my blood" are pronounced, the Son of God, in whose name these words are spoken, becomes present on earth in the flesh he once received from his Mother, the Virgin Mary. The Eucharist confers a new currency on the Incarnation.

The bond between the Incarnation and the Eucharist appears in a special manner in the Gospel of Saint John. The Prologue of this Gospel presents us with the Word who became flesh (see John 1:14). Subsequently, the Evangelist reports to us Jesus' words in the discourse of the proclamation of the Eucharist: "The bread that I will give for the life of the world is my flesh" (John 6:51). The use of the word "flesh" to indicate the Incarnation, and then the Eucharist, is pregnant with meaning. Jesus seems to have used the word "flesh," an authentic Semitic term, in his institution of the Eucharist; subsequently that word was translated into Greek with the word for "body" instead of "flesh." Thus, the disciples heard Jesus declare, "This [is] my flesh." The Latin word for flesh, *carn-*, is the root of the word "incarnation," and thus suggests a close bond between the mystery of the coming of Christ into this world and the mystery of the Eucharist.

When the Word descended to earth, "becoming flesh," he had the intent not only to lead a life parallel to our own, but also to offer that flesh for the life of the world. Thus, the Incarnation finds its completion in the Eucharist. The Eucharist confers on the Incarnation an import that the simple fact of the coming of Christ into the milieu of his earthly existence could not have had. It grants the flesh of the Son of God a power of radiance, as it were, that penetrates all of those who, in their own human flesh, are called to share the divine filiation and to live as children of the Father. To the highest degree, it offers the transforming power of the flesh of Christ, as that power must be exercised in the universal development of grace in all human existence.

This constitutes a response to the ready lament of those who understand the immense value of the Incarnation and have not had the privilege of living at that unique moment in the history of humanity. Those born after the death of Christ have not had the good fortune to know him. Jesus himself has called particular attention to the good fortune of his disciples: "Blessed are your eyes, for they see, and your ears, for they hear" (Matt. 13:16). We might have thought that this good fortune was that of only those who lived in Palestine during Jesus' earthly life. But the proclamation of this beatitude does not actually exclude those who are to live after him. It is predicated of all of those who in the past had awaited the Messiah and were not able to know him: "Many prophets and righteous people longed to see what you see, but did not see it, and to hear what you hear, but did not hear it" (Matt. 13:17).

To be sure, those born after Christ do not have the privilege granted to the Apostles, do not experience the visible presence of the Savior. They cannot have the experience that was possible only for a brief period of time and that was of unique value in history, the experience of the human proximity of the Son of God. But the sensible experience had by the disciples contained a spiritual experience: their good fortune did not consist only in seeing Jesus and hearing him. It included their discernment in him of the Son of God, for which faith is required. The eyes that saw and the ears that heard were those of believers, persons who had clung to Christ.

This higher beatitude, on the level of faith, is offered to all who recognize in Christ the Son of God come among us. It is offered through the revelation of the Gospel, which conveys a concrete understanding of the truth of the Incarnation. But it is especially offered through the Eucharist, in which the mystery of the Word made flesh is manifested and is endowed with an ever new currency. The Eucharist enables believers to welcome the presence of Christ as the contemporaries of Jesus were invited to welcome that presence long ago. It secures them the good fortune of seeing, with the eyes of faith, under a visible sign, Jesus' body and blood. As for a spiritual welcome of this presence, Christians of all times, through the Eucharist, receive the privilege that was offered to Jesus' contemporaries. They enjoy the good fortune of a most profound intimacy with the incarnate Son.

John Chrysostom, commenting on the passage in the Gospel of Matthew where we read that the inhabitants of Gennesaret brought Jesus their sick "and begged him that they might touch even the fringe of his cloak" (Matt. 14:36), says: "Let us, too, touch even the fringe of his cloak! Nay, if we will, we have Christ whole and entire. For his body is here before us now." And he continues: "Believe that this, now, is the table at which Jesus sat."[1]

Eucharist and Redemptive Sacrifice

Like the Incarnation, the Eucharist reproduces Jesus' redemptive offering. True, it does so sacramentally. According to the declaration reported by Saint John (see 6:51), the flesh of Christ is "given for the life of the world." It is not given only *to* the world, in order to cause a new life to blossom in believers; it is also given *for* the world, that is, offered in sacrifice in order to obtain that new life. Part and parcel of the redemptive sacrifice, it can feed humanity.

The allusion to sacrifice is more explicit in the words of consecration of the wine: "This is my blood of the covenant, which is poured out for many" (Mark 14:24). "For many," meaning, "for the multitude," is a Semitic expression used by Jesus and stating that his sacrifice is offered for humanity. "Many" can be understood as synonymous with "all." The intent to secure humanity a new life is the motive of the coming of the Savior on earth and of the sacrifice offered in the drama of Calvary. On the occasion of the Last Supper, Jesus' intent consisted not only in giving his flesh as food and his blood as drink to his disciples, but in giving it to them as fruit of the sacrifice destined to be to the benefit of all.

Every Eucharistic celebration renews this offering sacramentally. The words of consecration cause a mystical renewal of Jesus' sacrifice, that it may benefit humanity more broadly. To be sure, this offering is not made today as it was made in the beginning, with

---

1. *Homily on the Gospel of Matthew,* 50:2, PG 58:507.

the shedding of Christ's blood. It is made only through a sacramental rite. Still, it remains integral in its spiritual generosity. The entire personal offering of the Savior, with the totality of his sacrifice, is expressed in the Eucharistic offering.

Those who participate in the Eucharist are by that very fact engaged in a personal offering joined to that of Christ. The spirit of offering, which characterized Jesus' earthly life and reached its full development in his sacrifice, ought to inspire the life of Christians. While the painful aspects of human life could occasion the temptation to yield to a spirit of anxiety or faint-heartedness, the Eucharist arouses in those who share it a spirit of generous offering. Every Eucharistic celebration is a celebration of Christ's great "yes" to the Father — a "yes" that victoriously overcomes all of the "nos" inspired by sin.

It is important to emphasize that the Eucharist is not limited to the offering of sacrifice as it was accomplished on Calvary. Simultaneously, it commemorates the complement of that sacrifice in the mystery of the Resurrection. It is the vehicle of the mystery that is the wellspring of a higher life.

The body of Christ offered in sacrifice in the Eucharist is not his body in its earthly state. It is the body that has now attained its definitive state in the Resurrection. By virtue of his power of rising from death, the Savior repeats his deed of offering in the Eucharist through the mediation of the priest. When his body is given as food and his blood as drink, the body and blood are animated by a life-giving power attaching to them by virtue of the Resurrection, and then of the Ascension.

This is the reason why the Eucharist is celebrated in joy, even though it renews in us the sorrowful offering of Christ's Passion. The Passion is renewed with its inevitable issue in the triumph of the Resurrection. Even though it comes to us in the sorrowful context of sacrifice, through that very sacrificial offering the Eucharist gives us to share in the joy of the victory with which Christ emerged from the tomb and came to kindle once more the hearts of the disciples who were mourning his death (Luke 24:32).

Proclaiming to his disciples their participation in trial, Jesus guaranteed them their passage from sorrow to joy: "So you have pain now; but I will see you again, and your hearts will rejoice, and no one will take your joy from you" (John 16:22). Through the presence of the risen Christ, the Eucharist shows forth the constant fulfillment of this Gospel promise. The Eucharist demands participation in sacrifice, surely; but it does so the better to call forth the abundant, ultimate gladness that comes from the Resurrection. It perpetually recalls the truth that, together with a share in the redemptive sufferings of Christ, we are offered, as well, a participation in his triumph over evil and his communication of a loftier felicity.

Thus, the Eucharist furnishes a reply to the "whys" inevitably provoked by human sufferings. In the face of the most painful trials, as well as in comparatively minor sufferings, many are tempted to ask, resentfully, "Why?" The Eucharist replies, proving it by the gladness it secures for us, that suffering does not have the last word. The suffering of the Cross is not only our vessel of salvation; it also carries us to joy. In all suffering, then, is the promise of a greater gladness, which causes the wisdom and goodness of the divine design to appear in a better way. It is the spiritual experience alluded to, for example, in the *Acts of Thomas*, an ancient apocryphal writing venerated since the middle of the third century: "At daybreak," we read, "the Apostle Thomas broke the Eucharist, and made believers sharers in the table of Christ. They were happy, and full of gladness."[2]

By placing us on the highway of sacrifice, the Eucharist gives us the strength of offering, but at the same time offers us the guarantee of a deeper joy, of whose reality it gives us to taste here and now.

The Eucharist brings to light the fundamental nature of the Christian religion, which is a religion of the Cross, but also a religion of gladness. When he taught the Beatitudes, Jesus foretold most vividly the sorrowful journey that lay before his disciples, a journey whose primary sign would be persecution. The persecution that constantly beset the Master during his public life would be prolonged in the lives of his disciples. And yet the Beatitudes are a testimonial of joy. They promise a gladness that, far from being diminished or defeated by trial, is solidified and developed through

---

2. *Acts* 27, ed. Erbetta, 2:323.

sorrow. This joy is not promised just for life beyond the tomb. It is a joy that accompanies life on earth, although it will find its full development only in the life to come.

The Eucharist gives believers the strength to live the redemptive offering in a better way, but it does so by way of the strength that bestows the joy of the Resurrection, and does so with the aim of introducing believers more profoundly into the happiness announced by the Gospel. We understand, then, why the atmosphere of every Eucharistic celebration is an atmosphere of rejoicing and why Communion in the body and blood of Christ affords the ability to lead a more generous, but also more joyful, Christian life.

The Eucharist and the Transformation of Humanity

Eucharist and Gift of Grace

The Eucharist manifests the basic vision of the mystery of grace. "Grace" denotes a divine gift distinguished by its "gratuity." The grace that wells forth from Christ the Redeemer consists in the gift of divine life to humanity. For us the gift is gratuitous. But it was paid for at the highest price by our Savior.

The Eucharistic mystery makes it evident in the extreme that the entire new life granted human beings emerges from Christ, and that it is the very life of the Son of God that is communicated to all. "Those who eat my flesh and drink my blood have eternal life, and I will raise them up on the last day" (John 6:54), asserts Jesus, even before the institution of the Eucharist, in his first proclamation of the same. It was as if he were in haste to give his flesh and blood in order that everlasting life imbue his disciples and definitively assure their destiny. He specifies that, without the Eucharistic Communion, eternal life, which is the life of grace, is not given: "Very truly, I tell you, unless you eat the flesh of the Son of Man and drink his blood, you have no life in you" (John 6:53). Christ is the only source of divine grace for humanity. The Eucharistic meal, then, is the route par excellence of the distribution of grace: it is the condition for the development of the Christian life.

Since the Eucharist is the sacrament in which is given not only grace, but the author of grace, there is an exceptional link there with the entire life of grace. The presence of Christ's body and blood signifies a personal presence destined to make grace well up in limitless abundance.

We cannot conclude that the Eucharist is the source of the grace of the other sacraments, or the source of the entire life of grace. Christ alone is the source, and he is not this solely through the Eucharist. The Eucharist cannot be regarded as the channel through which pass all of the currents of grace. But it bestows the presence of Christ, who, in turn, is sovereign Lord of the distribution of grace. The one who willed to nourish humanity with his own life has chosen the Eucharist as a special means to reach to the very depths of human life and transform it into divine life.

This penetration is so powerful that it inscribes in the person a guarantee of final resurrection. Through Communion, Christians receive the absolute guarantee of this resurrection: their bodies of flesh are destined to bear within them Christ's eternal life. In furnishing this guarantee, the Eucharist secures for them the full effect of the mystery of the redemptive Incarnation, the effect of grace, the mystery of a divine life communicated to human flesh through the flesh of Christ.

Eucharist and Church

The Eucharist plays a determining role in the development of the Church. The Church is the assembly, the gathering effected by Christ through the Holy Spirit, the community that lives by his divine life. The assembly was born at the first Pentecost, and since then has never ceased to spread out to all peoples. Even in the very beginning, the life of the Christian community was expressed through "the breaking of the bread," that is, through the Eucharistic meal (see Acts 2:42). The "breaking of the bread" was regarded as a distinctive element in the Christian life of kinship.

Saint Paul, who sought to recall to the Corinthians the demands of unity and the need to put an end to all divisions, made appeal to the undeniable experience that is concretized in the Eucharist. After emphasizing that "the bread that we break" is a "sharing in the body of Christ," he declared: "Because there is one bread, we who are many are one body, for we all partake of the one bread" (1 Cor. 10:16–17). The meal at which Christ is offered as food not only joins to Christ each of those who share it; it also joins the participants with one another, since they are nourished by one food, and one which crowns them with an identical life.

The Eucharist not only constitutes a sign of unity, but also contributes to forming the unity of the Church. Christ, who gives his disciples to communicate in his body, models his community in his image. He undertakes and furthers a work of construction that intimately unites persons through one and the same faith and one love. The Eucharist celebrates the intimate union between Christ and his Church. Cyprian of Carthage writes, around the middle of the third century:

> When water is mixed with wine in the chalice, the people are united to Christ, and the multitude of the believers is bound and joined to him in whom they believe. This association and mingling of water and wine are so mixed in the chalice of the Lord that the mixture cannot be mutually separated. Whence nothing can separate the Church, that is, the multitude established faithfully and firmly in the Church, persevering in that which it has believed, from Christ as long as it clings and remains in undivided love.[3]

True, we have seen a reciprocal causality, according to which the Church produces the Eucharist and the Eucharist produces the Church. But in both cases, the origin of the production is always the activity of Christ: it is he who gives life to the Church, and who has originated and instituted the Eucharist.

The Church produces the Eucharist. It has received the mission to repeat, in memory of Christ, what was done at the Last Supper. In celebrating the Eucharist, the Church develops its community life: it is reinforced and increased as Church. It develops an activity of worship and prayer that sanctifies it and causes it to radiate into the world. It assumes more openly its mission of witness and of proclamation of the good news.

But the Eucharist produces the Church. Every Eucharistic celebration contributes to the formation of the Church, to the development of its holiness, and to the reinforcement of its unity. In the

---

3. *Letters*, 63, no. 13, trans. Rose Bernard Donna, *Saint Cyprian: Letters*, Fathers of the Church (Washington, D.C.: Catholic University of America Press, 1964), 211.

celebration of the mystery reproduced in his name, Christ perpetually joins human beings together into a Church and animates this Church with new strength for penetrating the universe.

In a very special manner, the Eucharist fosters the spiritual growth of the Church. There is an outer aspect in the Church, constituted of all of the visible manifestations of its presence and of its activity in the world. We are sometimes tempted to identify the Church with this earthly reality, and at other times we are tempted to see in it only its hierarchical structure.

The Eucharist tends to develop in the Church the interior life that inspires human hearts. It seeks to form, in all believers, a communion of soul that receives from Jesus Christ all of its strength and fervor. It seeks to foster the quality of the spiritual life, which is translated into a conduct that reflects that of Christ.

Among the demands of this quality of life, the Eucharist seeks to secure the development of prayer. With the gift of the presence of the body and blood of Christ, it shows the importance of openness and dialogue, the need of a sincere quest for oneness with the Savior. The mission of the Church cannot be carried out unless the Church is animated and sustained by a persevering prayer. The witness to which the members of the Church are called can be authentic only if it implies a fundamental adherence to the manner of activity and person of Christ.

Precisely this adherence of the whole person requires the continual coming of Christ in the Eucharist. This coming is necessary for the development of all of the missions of the Church. The Eucharist tends to render apostolic activity possible and efficacious, animating it with a spirit of essential communion with Christ. Its thrust is toward an interior construction that will be the guarantee of an authentic exterior edification or construction.

The attachment of the primitive Church to the "breaking of the bread" shows the essential value the first Christians attributed to the Eucharist for the development of the Christian community. This attachment derived from the memorial left by specific words of Jesus. With the growth of the Church, Christians can only continue to "devote themselves" to the Eucharist (see Acts 2:42).

In the Eucharist, the Church is strengthened in its testimonial of faith and charity. And so the priest prays:

God, Father of mercy,
grant us the Spirit of love, the Spirit of your Son.
Strengthen your people
with the Bread of Life and the Chalice of Salvation.
Make us perfect in faith and love,
in communion with our Pope and our Bishop.
Give us eyes to see
the needs and sufferings of our brothers and sisters.
Pour into us the light of your word
to comfort the weary and the oppressed:
grant that we may loyally devote ourselves
to the service of the poor and the suffering.
May your Church be a living witness
of truth and freedom, justice and peace,
that all men and women may open themselves to the hope of
a new world. (Eucharistic Prayer V/C)

The Eucharist in Our Personal Life

Eucharist and Faith

The exclamation in the liturgy "the mystery of faith!" recognizes
in the Eucharistic celebration an appeal to faith and a miracle of
faith. Christian faith is conscious of being challenged by a mystery
that enraptures it and transcends it. Only faith, with its openness to
the divine infinite, can accept the sacrificial offering effected with
the words "This is my body" and the presence deriving from them.

Faith in the Eucharist is not of a secondary order. It involves
the very essence of Christian revelation, since it presupposes faith
in a redemptive Incarnation and faith in the Church. Jesus had already accentuated the need for this faith on the occasion of the
first proclamation of the Eucharist. After the multiplication of the
loaves, he had commented on the miracle in order to reveal its true
import. He had declared that he had not come to give humanity an
abundance of material bread: he had come among human beings as
"the bread that came down from heaven" (John 6:58), and he was
bringing this bread to them. In a lengthy discourse pronounced in
the synagogue at Capernaum, he had revealed his intent to give his
flesh as food and his blood as drink. But he was met with disbelief

on the part of his audience. Even many of his disciples found the promise of the Eucharist unacceptable and abandoned the Master whom until then they had followed. This rejection of the promise of the Eucharist was surely a deep disappointment. But seeing his Apostles still there before him, impressed by this great testimonial of affection, he did not hesitate to demand from them the adherence of faith that he had not obtained from the great majority of his audience. He asked them, "Do you also wish to go away?" (John 6:67). He was prepared to let them leave unless they had believed in the Eucharist that he had just proclaimed. It seems evident, then, that it is not possible to follow Christ without believing in the Eucharist. Fortunately, Peter's profession in the name of all enabled the Apostles to continue to follow the Master. For Jesus, then, Christian faith can only be a Eucharistic faith. Acceptance of the Eucharist is an essential condition for acceptance of Christ. This cannot be ignored.

By virtue of this lively appeal to faith and to their loyalty to Jesus, the Apostles could receive the body and blood of Christ with a sincere, profound faith at the Last Supper. When they heard for the first time the words of Eucharistic consecration, they believed them, because, one year earlier, they had already made a personal option of faith in the promise of the Eucharist.

Subsequently, during the spread of the Church, this faith in the Eucharist remained the response to Christ's original invitation. In every celebration, always, Jesus continues to require the same faith. The Eucharist presents an altogether special problem. The contrast between what is visible in the bread and wine offered on the altar, and what is invisibly present, the body and blood of Christ, requires an ever renewed impetus of faith. It is a matter of overcoming the distance between what we perceive with our senses and what the truth of the mystery imposes upon our belief. But Christian faith always musters the courage to make this leap into the invisible.

Christian faith also finds its fundamental beatitude here — that which Jesus proclaimed when he sought to stimulate faith in the Resurrection and when he rebuked the blindness of the unbelief manifested by the Apostle Thomas: "Have you believed because you have seen me? Blessed are those who have not seen and yet

have come to believe" (John 20:29). The risen Lord has anticipated
and answered the objection of those who, in order to believe in the
presence of his living body in the Eucharistic mystery, would be
tempted to demand the opportunity to touch his pierced side and
to "put my finger in the mark of the nails" (John 20:25). Faith
detaches itself from sensible evidence by a loftier attachment to the
person of Jesus: this gives it the guarantee that it is truly "blessed,"
in the sense of "beatitude."

The darkness of faith, which keeps the Eucharist in the realm of
mystery, therefore does not prevent the welling up of the gladness
it provokes. The exclamation "The mystery of faith!" ever echoes
as a cry of joy: the joy of faith itself and the joy of the mystery that
is that of the risen Christ once more present amid humanity.

Eucharist and Charity

The Eucharist, mystery of faith, has also been regarded and lived
in the Church as a mystery of charity.

Faith itself is animated by charity. When Jesus called for a
commitment of faith during his public life, he was requiring a
movement of love that would unite persons to himself. He himself
recalled to a doctor of the law the value of the first commandment:
"You shall love the Lord your God with all your heart, and with all
your soul, and with all your might" (Deut. 6:5, Mark 12:30 and
parallels). As he revealed his divine person, that of the Son, this
commandment also demanded in his own regard a love that would
commit the whole heart, the whole soul, and all of one's might.
This exaction of a total love finds an application in the Eucharist:
the Eucharistic Christ asks to be received in Communion with this
love. Those whose food is the body of Christ must not consider it
only as food: they are invited to adore it, and love it with all their
heart, with all their soul, and with all their might. The love that
inspires the coming of Christ must be answered by the love of the
one who receives him.

When Jesus had enunciated the first commandment, he had
paired it expressly with the second: "You shall love your neighbor as yourself" (Lev. 19:18, Mark 12:31 and parallels). He also
broadened the outlook of this commandment with the parable
of the good Samaritan, abolishing the restrictions implicit in the

expression "your neighbor" and showing that all must become neighbors to their brothers and sisters (Luke 10:29–37). At the Last Supper, he communicates the whole import of the charity that he has come to inaugurate on earth. By way of a commentary on the Eucharist he is instituting, he enunciates his particular commandment, a "new commandment": "Just as I have loved you, you also should love one another" (John 13:34). This precept is the divine response to the division produced among the Apostles at the beginning of the Last Supper with their question as to which of them was the greatest (Luke 22:24).

Jesus had more than once been witness to disputes among the Twelve as to who would occupy the first positions in the future Reign. He did not limit himself to reproving his disciples: he ordered them to imitate the greatness of his own love. In giving himself as Eucharistic bread, he grants them the strength to make that imitation. He then proclaims the new law of charity, instilling in his disciples the capacity to follow it, in the power of the Eucharist.

To love as Christ has loved is a very high aim, attainable only by one who receives the divine strength of the love possessed by Christ himself. This divine force enables the Christian not only to overcome all tendencies to the selfishness and ambition that give rise to disputes, but to reach the very extremity of love's generosity, following the example given by the Savior in his sacrifice. By nourishing with the body and blood of Christ those who receive it, the Eucharist infuses them with the person of the incarnate Son, with all of the power of his love. And in this fashion it enables them to face all of the difficulties that arise along the path of charity and to overcome all obstacles.

In one of her poems, Saint Thérèse of the Child Jesus expresses the power of charity springing from the Eucharist as follows:

> Jesus, my sacred and holy Vine,
> O my divine King, you know me well,
> this withered bunch of grapes that I am,
> and you know that I must vanish for you.
> In the winepress of suffering,
> I shall prove to you my eternal love.

Naught will I here below
but to immolate myself day after day. (Poem 25)

More particularly, the Eucharist bestows on the one who is nourished by it the development of the manifold virtualities of love. Indeed, it is the heart of Christ that possesses the fullness of love: it is only he who reveals all of its secrets and assures its most complete development. By commanding his disciples to love one another as he had loved them, he was offering them not only a model, but also a wellspring, ever available, inexhaustible, of the love that gives itself to the limit. The words "as I have loved you" recall the love that reached its pinnacle in the sacrifice of the Cross. This same love, in every Christian life, must attain a summit of its own, in the offering of all that is painful and sorrowful.

At the Last Supper, by serving his disciples, Jesus better conveys the import of true love for others. When he began to wash his disciples' feet, presenting himself as the slave of them all, he bore impressive witness of the humility characteristic of love. Conscious of his divine sovereignty, a sovereignty he would presently declare in his trial before the council, he makes no appeal to his power in order to overwhelm or domineer, but simply serves. No one is as humble as he. With this humility, which he seeks to transmit to his disciples by urging them to wash one another's feet, he opens the way to the agreement of the heart, to the harmony that avoids the quarrels arising from self-love. Making himself the least of all, he shows us the manner in which all of those conflicts ought to be resolved in which human beings are tempted to try to have the upper hand.

In the Eucharist, Jesus' deed of humility is reproduced. Indeed, he abases himself to the point of becoming food and drink for those he loves. He who could have manifested himself in the splendor of his divine glory makes himself present in the lowliest of ways. He places himself at the service of humanity, feeding it with his body and slaking its thirst with his blood. Every Eucharistic celebration is a discreet manifestation of a humble love, of a love that desires to communicate itself to the world along with its humility.

Jesus himself conveys the fact that this spirit of service would find its expression in sacrifice: "The Son of Man came not to be served but to serve, and to give his life a ransom for many" (Mark 10:45, Matt. 20:28). Humble service is expressed in the most extreme manner in the offering of sacrifice: the Son of Man, he who, although a human being, is a divine person, offers himself as a ransom, in the most complete humiliation, in order to obtain the deliverance of humanity.

As he explains to his disciples, inviting them to follow his example, sacrifice is the greatest deed of love: "No one has greater love than this, to lay down one's life for one's friends" (John 15:13). In the face of the supreme demand of the gift of life, we could cower. Jesus knows this — he who in Gethsemane had the temptation to shrink from death. Still, he asks his disciples to imitate him in the commitment that led him to Calvary itself. With the Eucharist just celebrated, he had furnished them with the strength they needed in order to follow him along the pathway of sacrifice.

The Eucharist responds to every kind of fear that could arise in the face of the sorrowful way of the Passion. It supplies Christians the thrust of love necessary to accept trials and make an offering of them. By communicating to every disciple the generous life of Christ, it renders them capable of giving themselves without reserve and with total availability. It opens the soul to all of the exigencies of love, and gives new vigor to that soul's fervor in the face of the sufferings of life. The Eucharist causes charity to blossom through sacrifice, strengthening the secret gladness of this love.

Eucharist and Hope

The Eucharist shows itself extremely rich in the most authentic hope — in hope for the destiny of humanity and of each individual as such.

With regard to the life of the individual, it is Jesus himself who reveals this hope, as he proclaims: "Those who eat my flesh and drink my blood have eternal life, and I will raise them up on the last day" (John 6:54). It is the eternal life of Christ that penetrates the soul of one who receives the Eucharistic flesh and blood, and this gift of eternal life guarantees the resurrection that will take place at the end of the world.

With regard to the destiny of humanity, the proclamation of

the coming of Christ into the world, which opens the entire outlook of the future of humanity, is taken up and broadened by
the Eucharist, as Saint Paul says: "As often as you eat this bread
and drink the cup, you proclaim the Lord's death until he comes"
(1 Cor. 11:26). Thus, the Eucharist contributes an essential element
for Christ's glorious return.

This coming can be understood in the broadest sense. That is, it
is a coming which is initiated by the first assembly of the Church
at Pentecost, is continued in the current existence of the world, and
will be completed when all of the work of evangelization has been
brought to a completion, that is, at the end of the world (see Matt.
24:14).

To use the words of Ignatius to the Ephesians, the Eucharist is
the "drug of immortality, the antidote for death, for living ever in
Jesus Christ" (20, 2).

The Eucharist possesses an essential eschatological value. It
proclaims the characteristics of the last days and is one of the guarantees that they will come. It brings Christians hope and bestows
on this hope the strength to realize its object.

By introducing Christ into the Christian community, the Eucharist cooperates in his coming, throughout the universe, and in
the work of the spread of the Church. It secures for those charged
with evangelization the spiritual strength they need. It directs all of
the future toward its crowning moment, when the coming of Christ
will have reached its maximal expansion and will have realized,
with the end of the world, the general resurrection.

The Eucharist sends communities and individuals down the road
to their final destiny. It is an inexhaustible spring of hope, of a hope
that does not disappoint (see Rom. 5:5), because it is fastened to
the sovereign power of Christ and to the immensity of his love,
which is poured out for us to overflowing through the Holy Spirit.

Thanksgiving

A résumé of the value and importance of the Eucharist in Christian
life affords us a recognition of the marvelous wealth of the divine
ingenuity and inventiveness. More particularly, it conveys to us a
better understanding of the basis of the term "Eucharist," which

means "Thanksgiving." In Christ, the Eucharist was animated by his thanksgiving to the Father. It brings us to this basic disposition of thanksgiving and to an appreciation of the divine gifts. In these gifts are manifested the sovereign wisdom of the whole divine design of salvation and the goodness that pours forth the benefits of the sacramental presence of Christ, his sacrifice, and his meal, for the growth of the Church and of each and every Christian. The Eucharist develops faith, love, and hope, thus conferring plenitude upon the returning of thanks, which brings to its extreme point the thrust of gratitude rising to the Father for his infinite love.

Chapter 2

Origin of the Eucharist

Witness of Saint Paul

The importance of the Eucharist is attested with the vigor of Saint Paul's appeal to the most primitive tradition, from which he has this truth. The Eucharist is a marvel that could appear unbelievable, were it not guaranteed by the faithful tradition of a record that, beyond any doubt, goes back to Christ himself.

Chronologically, the testimonial of the First Letter to the Corinthians is the most ancient. The letter was written around A.D. 56–57, so that its witness is older than that of the Gospels. But antiquity aside, we must take note of the fact that Paul indicates Jesus himself as origin of the tradition reported by him, for the sake of a powerful emphasis on the indubitable authenticity of the truth being transmitted.

> For I received from the Lord what I also handed on to you, that the Lord Jesus on the night when he was betrayed took a loaf of bread, and when he had given thanks, he broke it and said, "This is my body that is for you. Do this in remembrance of me." In the same way he took the cup also, after supper, saying, "This cup is the new covenant in my blood. Do this, as often as you drink it, in remembrance of me."
>
> (1 Cor. 11:23–25)

From this fact, based on the secure witness of tradition, Paul deduces a conclusion regarding the essential meaning of the Eucharistic meal: "For as often as you eat this bread and drink the cup, you proclaim the Lord's death until he comes" (1 Cor. 11:26). The circumstances of this meal, which took place the night Jesus was betrayed, and the meaning of the words referring to the body offered for the disciples and the blood poured out in the new covenant, shed light on the magnitude of a meal whose purpose was to proclaim the death of Christ, with a view to his coming in glory.

"I Received from the Lord..."

The expression "I received from the Lord" does not mean that Paul had a special revelation in which Christ himself had addressed him. What he has received is a tradition having its origin in the actions and words of Jesus. He transmits that tradition to the Corinthians, in full awareness that the validity of the tradition was guaranteed not only by the recollections of those who had passed the tradition on to him, but also by the actual authority of Christ, who instituted the Eucharist. Paul seeks to underscore the fact that the teaching transmitted by his Eucharistic catechesis does not come from a simple opinion or from a personal interpretation: the testimonial he offers has been received entirely from the doctrine that is transmitted in the Church. He has simply taken the truth that has been attested by certain witnesses of the Last Supper and faithfully preserved by those who have received their recollections, recollections which they agree go back to Christ himself as source of the Eucharist.

This solemn appeal to tradition on Paul's part is verified in another context, apropos of the resurrection of Christ. In the same Letter to the Corinthians, we are struck by an analogous insistence on the transmission that guarantees the authenticity of the faith: "I handed on to you as of first importance what I in turn had received: that Christ died for our sins in accordance with the scriptures" (1 Cor. 15:3). Christ's redemptive death and resurrection are the content of the most fundamental assertion of Christian revelation. More particularly, the Resurrection is the miracle par excellence confirming the whole teaching given by Jesus and manifesting the victorious spiritual might with which he communicates to humanity salvation and new life, his very life, ordained to transform the existence of all individuals. This event, like the Eucharist, must be guaranteed by a tradition founded on the experiences of the first witnesses.

It is significant that Paul appeals expressly to the guarantee of tradition for two declarations of faith, that of the drama of Easter — Jesus' death and resurrection — and that of the Eucharist. Thereby he wishes to suggest that the Eucharist is an essential truth, of the greatest importance, bound up with the accomplishment of the work of salvation. In this work, Christ's death and resurrection form an apex, realized in the events of history. In the area of Christian worship, an analogous importance attaches to the Eucharist: the Eucharist introduces into the life of the believer the transformative fecundity of the Savior's death and resurrection.

Furthermore, Paul explicitly and emphatically insists on the first origins of the tradition relative to the Eucharist when he says, "I received from the Lord." For the tradition relative to the Resurrection, he limits himself to saying, "I in turn had received." Indeed this tradition arises from the testimony of the Apostles, who had seen the living Christ: in reality, the first witness had been that of the women who had been the first to encounter the Risen One, but had acquired formal authority only after it had been received and confirmed by the Apostles. Apropos of the Eucharist, the tradition is received directly from the Lord, because it was the words and action of Christ that instituted the Eucharist at the Last Supper, with the formal invitation to reproduce the mystery celebrated for the first time on the eve of the redemptive drama: "Do this in memory of me."

Thus, the tradition received from the Lord means not only a transmission of recollections guaranteed by witnesses, but also a transmission of the will of Christ that continues to guide the Church by associating it to his death and resurrection in the Eucharistic mystery. It is a tradition guaranteeing Jesus' active intervention in every Eucharistic celebration. He who had created and instituted the Eucharist continues, through the intervention of his Church, to make an offering through the gift of his body and blood. It is a matter of an action on the part of the "Lord," that is, according to the meaning attributed to this word by Saint Paul, of Christ in the full possession of all of his saving power.

"Do This in Memory of Me"

Paul has preserved for us this addendum pronounced by Jesus after the consecration of the bread and then that of the wine. This same order marks the celebration of the Eucharist in the Church. Luke places the injunction immediately after the consecration of the bread (Luke 22:19), before going on to report that of the wine

(Luke 22:20), while Paul places it after the consecration of the wine, so that as a result it refers to both consecrations.

This order has had notable consequences, not only for the repetition of the Eucharistic celebration, but also for the choice of what absolutely had to be repeated in the celebration itself. The Apostles understood that Jesus' intent was a repetition both of the consecration of the bread and that of the cup, with the invitation to eat his body and drink his blood. The two consecrations gave a new meaning to two rites of the Passover meal: the initial blessing of the bread and, toward the end, the blessing reserved for the cup. All the rest of the Supper was allowed to disappear in the Christian liturgy. The words "Do this in memory of me" clearly indicated what must be done in order for the memory of Christ to be actualized as he willed. Therefore Christian worship has not reproduced the consumption of the Passover lamb, but only the double consecration of the bread and the wine.

This twin consecration takes up the two corresponding rites of the Jewish meal, while profoundly transforming their meaning and conferring upon them a new value. The novelty derives from the redemptive sacrifice, which confers a higher content on the meal. The blessing of the bread in use in the Jewish liturgy allowed the bread to retain its consistency, and destination for bodily nourishment, while the consecration pronounced by Jesus changes the bread into his body for spiritual nourishment. In the same manner, the cup of blessing provided an actual wine to be passed among the guests, while in the Christian liturgy, through the consecration, it becomes the cup of the Savior's blood, and is ordained to communicate, along with the supreme love animating the blood spilled for humanity, a spiritual inebriation.

The Apostles were to do something basically new, then, something infinitely superior to all that early liturgies had been able to imagine and celebrate. The magnitude of the novelty is expressed in the words "in memory of me." The Passover meal was solemnized in memory of Yahweh, the sovereign God who had manifested his power by delivering the Hebrew people from the yoke of Egypt. This God was offered the homage of the people's gratitude and admiration for the marvel of his liberating intervention. Jewish worship recalled, for all time, the miraculous deed by which God had saved his people. They found in it an essential motive of praise and adoration.

This concentration of regard and homage, entirely directed toward God, henceforth must be directed to Christ. The new meal is to be celebrated "in memory" of the "I" that is Jesus: the "I" of a human being, but at the same time, and especially, the "I" of the one who is God. Indeed, this is the "I" of the one who has revealed his proper identity by saying, "I am." It is a matter of a divine "I" belonging to eternity, and ruling over all human time, more especially all of the past of the Jewish people, as declared in the assertion: "Very truly, I tell you, before Abraham was, I am" (John 8:58).

Jesus had an awareness that his "I" was a divine "I." His mysterious person was an eternal person. In commanding his disciples to repeat the act of the Eucharist in memory of him, he was only acknowledging with respect to his own "I" the sovereign position it occupied in the work of salvation. His "I" was that of the Son of God, and as such was to play a unique role in the destiny of humanity. As he had existed from all eternity, so also he would never cease to exist and to constitute the Center that would attract to itself the thrust of faith, of prayer, and of love for all humanity. Every Eucharistic celebration renews the memory of the "I" of Christ. It guides minds and hearts toward the person of the incarnate Son of God.

Memorial

In saying, "Do this in memory of me," Jesus not only desired that human beings living after him should remember him. He wished to make the Eucharist a memorial.

The memorial is defined by its objective reality. It does not consist simply in a subjective memory — a recollection that is reality only in thought. It is an external, institutional manifestation of memory: it is a recollection definitively inscribed in history, that it may give a perpetual character to the event to be commemorated.

The Passover meal, then, was a memorial, an institution annually recalling the deliverance granted by God to his people. This memorial was the guarantee that the Exodus, an event of the past, would return to the memory of the Jews and reinforced their attachment to the God of their liberation.

With the Eucharist, Jesus has willed a new memorial. By transforming the Passover meal into the Eucharistic meal, he instituted a memorial that would everlastingly reproduce what occurred at the Last Supper. It did not suffice that the sublime love inspiring his redemptive Passion should remain in humanity's recollection. This love sought to give itself in a meal destined to be shared in the life of the Church and providing an everlasting renewal of the redemptive offering.

This was the guarantee of the objective reality of the memorial. Jesus had the power to give this memorial a supreme value, because he himself was God and possessed, in the eternity of his divine person, a total sovereignty over the passage of time. He was able to render present and current that which had been an event of the past: and thus he was able to repeat, without end, as time went on for his Church, his deed of the moment of the institution of the Eucharist. We must further observe that the invitatio, "Do this" cannot conceal the more fundamental truth of the divine initiative and action in the Eucharist: through the mediation of the one who "does this," the priest, it is Christ who acts. It is he who offers and bestows himself.

The Eucharistic memorial is unique in its kind, by reason of the divinity of Christ: here, memory and actual presence coincide. There exists one sole recollection of the sacrifice accomplished once and for all for the salvation of humanity: this sacrifice, whenever it is commemorated, becomes current and actual once again as a sacramental reality. In the same fashion, there is far more here than a simple recollection of the meal taken by Jesus with his Apostles on the eve of his death: in its Eucharistic value, this meal is reproduced with the presence of the body and blood of the Savior.

The memorial concretely revives the recollection of the Last Supper and stimulates us to admiration of the divine ingenuity and creativity, here implemented in order to introduce humanity more profoundly into the mystery of the redemptive Incarnation. It arouses a stronger attachment to the person of Christ.

Jesus had proclaimed this power of attraction that he would exercise upon all human beings: "I, when I am lifted up from the

earth, will draw all people to myself" (John 12:32). When the
words echo in the Eucharistic celebration, "Do this in memory of
me!" this universal attraction that proceeds from Christ's "I" is renewed. The Savior has been lifted up from the earth, first on the
Cross, and then in glory through the Ascension. His painful lifting up on the Cross, and then his glorious exaltation in celestial
glory, are commemorated in the Eucharist with the aim of ensuring
a broader influence of the Savior's power, which unites humanity
around his own person.

In rendering present this "I" of Christ through the gift of his
body and blood, the Eucharist discharges its function as a memorial. This memorial is rich in a past consummated in the heroic
offering of an "I" sacrificed for the benefit of all. It contains
the guarantee of a future expressed through an increase of the
gathering of the Christian community in the universe.

The Gospel Testimonials

Besides the witness of Paul on the institution of the Eucharist, we
have that of the three Gospels of Mark, Matthew, and Luke. The
four accounts of this institution present slight differences from one
another, but we can say that they substantially coincide in their
way of recounting the event and of reporting Jesus' words. This
agreement does not derive from the influence of Paul — whose account is chronologically older in its redaction and diffusion — since
those of Mark and Matthew have a Semitic form that seems more
primitive.

Indeed, two forms of the account of the institution have developed independently of each other. On the one side we have that
recounted by Mark and followed by Matthew; on the other, there
is the form recounted by Paul, which has influenced the Lukan
account. Being more Semitic, the Markan and Matthean version
seems closer to its roots, more literally faithful to the words pronounced by Jesus. Still, in its essential fidelity, Paul's version is no
less solidly attested by the tradition from which it emerges, although it does manifest a greater adaptation to the language and
culture of the Greek milieu. Especially, it has an order of repetition that can have been included only because it came from Jesus

himself. That order has not been adopted in Mark and Matthew, probably because in their tradition it was taken for granted: the Eucharist could be celebrated only by imitation of what Christ had done at the Last Supper. The fact remains that, on this point, the tradition reported by Paul is more complete — more integrally faithful to the event and to the words pronounced by Jesus.

It is not a matter, then, of receiving a form of the account of the institution as if it were the sole valid one. The four accounts that we have can help us better to rediscover the authentic origin of the Eucharist. Each has a value of its own.

Markan (14:22-25) and Matthean (26:26-29) Version

The accounts of the institution of the Eucharist in Mark and in Matthew are very similar. In Matthew we observe a slight amplification vis-à-vis Mark, but the essentials of the account are identical.

Invitation to the Meal. The version of Mark and Matthew includes an invitation to eat: "Take" (Mark); "Take, eat" (Matthew). This invitation is absent in the accounts of Paul and Luke, but it surely corresponds to Jesus' intent, since, when he took the bread, saying, "This is my body," he wished to give his own body as food. Even in the case that this expression of invitation were not to have been pronounced as reported to us, nevertheless it is implicit in the words and the gesture of consecration, which transmit the intent that the body of Christ be given as authentic spiritual food.

In Mark's account, the invitation is not repeated for the cup, while the Matthean account contains the words "Drink from it, all." The emphasis falls on a universal participation. In the context of the Last Supper, the invitation is addressed to all of the disciples, and in the subsequent Eucharistic context, when the Eucharist is celebrated by the priest, the invitation is addressed to all believers, to all of the faithful there present. The universal character of the invitation harmonizes altogether particularly with the words of consecration of the wine, which declare that the blood of Christ is shed for the multitude, that is, for all human beings. Since the sacrifice of the Savior is offered for all humanity, all human beings are invited to take part in the Eucharistic meal at which Christ's blood is given as drink.

The invitation to eat, and then to drink, has the effect of calling attention to Christ's desire to nourish believers with his body and to slake their thirst with his blood. It is he who organizes the Eucharistic banquet, and it is he who personally invites all persons to take advantage of it. The invitation resembles the one addressed by the king who has set a table for the wedding of his son: "Everything is ready; come to the wedding banquet" (Matt. 22:4). With his invitation, the Son is doing "what he sees the Father doing"; what the Father does, "the Son does likewise" (John 5:19).

"My Blood of the Covenant." "This is my blood of the covenant, which is poured out for many" (Mark 14:24, Matt. 26:28).

The version of Mark and Matthew differs from that of Paul and Luke especially in the words accompanying the consecration of the cup. The assertion is more direct, "This is my blood," while in Paul and Luke it is expressed in a more complex manner: "This cup is the new covenant in my blood."

The version of Mark and Matthew, more simple, is also closer to the formula of the striking of God's covenant with the Hebrew people reported in Exodus. Sprinkling the people with the blood of animal sacrifices, Moses had declared: "See the blood of the covenant that the Lord has made with you in accordance with all these words" (Exod. 24:8). Jesus adopts this formula, thereby demonstrating the performance of a rite that in the Old Testament could only have had a prefigurative value. He adopts it, but adds an essential qualification: "This is my blood of the covenant," or, more literally, "This is the blood of me, of the covenant."

Christ is not only the one who realizes the covenant foretold by the Hebrew prophets: he *is* the covenant, struck at the price of his blood. Indeed, if he is mediator between God and humanity, the reason is that he is personally both God and a human being. In him is realized the covenant in all of its breadth and in a manner transcending all that has been said in the past concerning the new covenant that God wished to establish. God and a human being in a single person, Christ represents, on the one hand, God in the divine relations of friendship with humanity and, on the other, humanity in its reconciliation with God by way of sacrifice. The true, definitive covenant, then, hinges on the person of the incarnate Son of God: in him, the union between divinity and humanity assumes a unique and perfect form

His Blood Spilled for Many. While Paul's version limits itself to asserting the presence of the blood, Matthew's specifies that the blood is offered in sacrifice.

Christ's blood is poured out "for many," "for the multitude" — that is, for the whole of humanity. The covenant is struck by way of sacrifice: the mystery of the Incarnation itself would not have sufficed. Owing to the sins of humanity, the covenant assumes a character of reconciliation, with an essential aspect of expiation, whose suggestive image is that of blood poured forth. This blood, which belongs to the Son of God, obtains, through its spilling, and more specifically through the generous love inspiring the offering, the salvation of the "multitude" — of the whole of humanity. This is the blood that is offered as drink. Besides the efficacy of the sacrifice for all human beings, there is also an efficacy of the meal for those who share in the Eucharist. To drink the blood of Christ means to enter into the mystery of the redemptive sacrifice, through a most intimate union with the Savior.

The formula used in the consecration of the wine recalls the explanation furnished by Jesus of his coming on earth: "The Son of Man came not to be served but to serve, and to give his life a ransom for many" (Mark 10:45, Matt. 20:28). His mission consisted essentially in a service, a service that would culminate in sacrifice. Speaking of a ransom, Jesus made allusion to the supreme expiatory sacrifice, intended to obtain forgiveness for humanity's transgressions.

As we see, the idea of a ransom poured out for the multitude requires the premise of a close bond between Christ and the covenant. As the representative of all human beings, Jesus acquired salvation for them, together with the divine life given to overflowing. It is he who, in the name of all, offers the sacrifice, and thus transforms the destiny of every single individual.

Those called to share in the Eucharistic meal must not forget the primordial fact that the blood they are invited to drink is that of a more integral sacrifice. Saint Paul's formulation, which is limited to speaking of the covenant in the blood, likewise makes allusion to sacrifice. This sacrificial reference is also confirmed by the words:

"As often as you eat this bread and drink the cup, you proclaim the Lord's death" (1 Cor. 11:26). It is as fruit of the sacrifice that the meal at which the blood of Christ is offered as drink acquires all of its value. That blood possesses a value all the more precious as it is poured out for the multitude.

Thus, the sacrifice contributes to the attributes of the meal. The red wine served at the Passover meal was appropriate for evoking the notion of blood. In a context of the Jewish rite, it recalled the blood of the Passover lamb; in a perspective of the first Eucharist, it testified that Christ, henceforth the Passover lamb par excellence, was giving his own blood as drink.

The Covenant. In the formula of the consecration of the wine, did Jesus speak of a covenant, or of a new covenant? According to Mark and Matthew, he calls his blood the blood of the covenant, while according to Paul and Luke he declares that the cup is the new covenant in his blood. The difference may seem of little importance or significance. Still, it helps us to a better understanding of the thought of Christ at the moment of the institution of the Eucharist. One of the most characteristic properties of Jesus' language, simplicity, leads us to prefer the expression "covenant," simply. We are also inclined to think that the expression "the new covenant" was probably added by Christians who desired to underscore the distance between the Hebrew covenant and the Christian. Besides, the more ancient origin of the version of Mark and Matthew encourages us to regard the simple mention of "covenant" as being more primitive.

In using this expression without further qualifying it, Jesus wished to convey that he himself was the most authentic covenant. Indeed, he is the only real covenant. The covenants recalled in the Old Testament are nothing but prefigurations of the one definitive covenant that God had the intention of striking with humanity. The covenants with the Hebrew people were efficacious only in view of Christ, of whom they were the prefiguration. When the reconciliation of sinners with God occurred in those covenants, and the wiping away of transgressions, the divine forgiveness was granted only in anticipation of the future event of the redemptive sacrifice.

Those who have attributed to Jesus the identification with the new covenant have thereby expressed what had been implied with respect to succession in time, counterpoising the new covenant against the old. Or else they have applied to Jesus the inauguration of a "new covenant" on the basis of Jeremiah's prophecy (Jer. 31:1). The expression has a legitimate sense, since in any case, even speaking simply of a "covenant," Jesus meant a new covenant, which introduced a new order of grace for humanity.

Still, we think, Jesus preferred the simpler expression, "the covenant," as more suitable and richer in meaning. He did not take the viewpoint of the course of history and its successive eras. He saw his task in function of the whole life of humanity.

Jesus is the unique covenant for all times, since he alone unites humanity with the Father and makes the Father's merciful goodness available to human beings who have need of forgiveness. His blood is offered as drink as a perpetual covenant in all Eucharistic celebrations, multiplied throughout the world.

The expression used in the liturgy, "new and everlasting covenant," reveals what Jesus meant with the single word, "covenant." The covenant is new because it is identified with Christ. Thus it is fundamentally different from the covenant inaugurated in the Hebrew religion, which had a value of preparation and prefiguration alone. The covenant of which Jesus speaks is new with the very newness of God, who has been revealed in the redemptive Incarnation.

The covenant is everlasting not only because it is destined to abide forever and guide the future of humanity, but also because, by virtue of the divine eternity, it flows back into all of the past, covering the whole duration of human history from beginning to end. Through this covenant, Christ our Redeemer introduces human beings into the eternity of heaven, an eternity that will infinitely overspill the end of the world.

Through communion in the blood of Christ, the Eucharist steeps human life in the new and everlasting covenant. This is the unique covenant, definitively fixing human destiny on its highest possible level.

"For the Forgiveness of Sins." In the formula of the consecration of the wine, only Matthew's account contains the expression "for the forgiveness of sins" (Matt. 26:28). These words are in-

tended to indicate more clearly the aim of the expression "blood,
...which is poured out for many." We are dealing with an expiatory sacrifice — a sacrifice offered to obtain the remission of sins.
This kind of sacrifice was practiced in Jewish worship, where it
played a very important role.

Here it is a matter of a sacrifice that is unique, since in place
of animals as sacrificial victims it is not only a human life that is
offered, but that of the divine person of the Son of God, just as
it is he who offers the sacrifice. He voluntarily commits himself to
death in order to obtain forgiveness for the multitude of human
beings. Thus the expiatory sacrifice takes on astonishing dimensions and, especially, reveals the gravity of humanity's sin. It is this
sin, indeed, that, by the free decision of the divine sovereignty, has
entailed the offering of the sacrifice.

Did Jesus actually pronounce these words? There is no certain
answer to this question. Actually, to have done so would have suggested that the sole aim of the sacrifice was the remission of sins,
while in fact it was broader: through his sacrifice, Jesus wished to
obtain for human beings the gift of everlasting life — the Good
Shepherd "lays down his life for the sheep" that they may "have
life, and have it abundantly" (John 10:10–11).

Nevertheless, it is certain that the sacrifice of Calvary was intended to communicate this more abundant life by securing the
remission of sins. The words reported by the Matthean version,
then, express an essential truth: the victory won by Christ over the
forces of evil. These words recall that the world is a sinful world,
but one that has been saved. Every Eucharistic celebration is thus
stronger than all of the evil of the world. Those who would be inclined to be impressed, indeed discouraged, by the manifestations
of evil in the universe find in the Eucharist a response to their feelings of sorrow. The Eucharist renews the Savior's definitive victory
over all of the forces of evil and communicates, in abundance, a life
of love whose bestowal is accompanied by the remission of sins.

Luke's Version (22:19–20)

Words of Institution. With respect to the words pronounced by
Jesus in the institution of the Eucharist, Luke's version coincides
with that of Paul, but with more stress on the intention of sacrifice.

In the consecration of the bread, Paul's brief formula, "This is my body that is for you," is replaced by "This is my body, which is given for you." Still, we observe that it is most probable that, with the simplicity of a language charged with meaning, Jesus expressed himself as Paul reports, limiting his words to "for you," or else, in parallel with the formula used for the wine, "for many." In fact, the expression "for you" seems to have a particular application to the community present, unlike the more general formula, "for many." In the sacrifice offered for the multitude, it was important to recognize the generosity of the gift, and this is what the Lukan text does: the body is "given," first and foremost, not as food, but as a gift for the benefit of all.

In the same way, in the consecration of the cup, while Paul limits himself to defining it as "the new covenant in my blood," Luke adds, "poured out for you." He makes this addition at the price of a difficult grammatical agreement, a sign that he was very concerned to complete a Pauline formula that he regarded as too brief. The blood is poured out for the multitude, and therefore for the participants in the supper, just as the body is given for them. The reference to sacrifice affords us an understanding of the gift of the body and blood in their just value.

Eschatological Climate. Luke's text involves difficulties of interpretation, inasmuch as, before the words of the institution of the Eucharist, it includes two other declarations, relating to the Passover supper.

> When the hour came, he took his place at the table, and the apostles with him. He said to them, "I have eagerly desired to eat this Passover with you before I suffer; for I tell you, I will not eat it until it is fulfilled in the kingdom of God." Then he took a cup, and after giving thanks he said, "Take this and divide it among yourselves; for I tell you that from now on I will not drink of the fruit of the vine until the kingdom of God comes." (Luke 22:14–18)

How are these two pronouncements to be understood, and what is their specific link with the institution of the Eucharist? We can say that they constitute the eschatological climate of the Paschal meal. The first declaration was pronounced at the beginning of the meal, and the second probably at the end. Both have been reported by Luke before the account of the institution, since they are in close connection with each other, although the first precedes the institution and the other follows it.

In the first, Jesus expresses an intense desire to celebrate this meal. It is his last Passover meal before his Passion. He desires it altogether particularly as a meal that will find a complement in the Reign of God. It is this complement that he is in haste to realize: he will realize it with the Eucharist that will be celebrated in his Reign, that is, in the Church.

It is a matter of an eschatological complement: the inauguration of the Reign of God belongs to the last times. The Eucharist will be an earthly repast, in which the heavenly food will be given human beings for the development of a Reign that is to spread throughout the world and prepare the initiation of definitive joy.

Let us note the accent placed by Jesus on his personal desire to inaugurate the Eucharist. The Semitic expression "With desire have I desired" (Luke 22:15) denotes a profound desire that involves the whole person. It is persons who have need of the Eucharistic meal, but it is Christ who feels a desire for it, even more than they. The enunciation of this desire is intended to arouse our own desire. Implicitly, it is an inquiry addressed to all Christians as to their desire to share in the Eucharist and their desire to communicate in it.

The second eschatological declaration is made at the moment of the last cup. Since the Passover meal included four cups, this one would have been the fourth. The third, called the Cup of Blessing, could not have been the one preceded by this declaration, since Jesus asserts that henceforth he will no longer drink of the fruit of the vine: only the last cup could have been the occasion of that prediction. Besides, Jesus could not have drunk the fourth, consecrated, cup containing the Eucharistic wine. The communion in his blood could only have been an act performed by his disciples.

Hence, only after the fourth cup of the Passover meal would the inauguration of the Reign of God take place.

This demonstrates the bond of the Eucharist with the coming of the Reign, that is, with the development of the Church, the gate of access to the Reign of heaven.

Testimony of John

The Gospel of John has no account of the institution of the Eucharist. We may wonder why the Evangelist did not hand down an account that has such a great importance in the teaching of Paul and of the Synoptic Gospels.

The essential reason for this silence will be found, it seems, in the intention of the Evangelist, who sought to complete the information given by the other Gospels and who considered the words and deeds with which Jesus had instituted the Eucharistic rite to have been amply attested by them. Besides, this was an altogether familiar rite, as it continued to be reproduced in the Christian communities.

The Gospel of John contains two essential additions to the teachings furnished by the other Gospels regarding the account of the institution. First and foremost, John reports the first proclamation of the Eucharist, in the synagogue at Capernaum after the miracle of the multiplication of the loaves. The very manner in which he reports the miracle, recalling that Jesus had taken the loaves and "given thanks" (John 6:11), suggested the prayer as the origin of the name "Eucharist." In the discourse pronounced in order to reveal the meaning of the miracle (John 6:26–28), Jesus manifested his intent to give his body as food and his blood as drink — a very decided intention in view of the fact that he declares the necessity of this meal if one is to have everlasting life. Furthermore, in defining that he was the bread of life come down from heaven, he underscores the relationship between the Eucharist and the Incarnation. He specifies as well that his body and blood would be given in their glorious state, in which they would be crowned with the life of the Spirit (John 6:61–63). In this fashion, he sheds light on the essential meaning of the Eucharistic meal.

In addition, we might understand the sacrificial element of the meal on the basis of the words "The bread that I will give for the life of the world is my flesh" (John 6:51). We are in the presence of an assertion very closely akin to the formula of the consecration of the bread, since "that I will give for the life of the world is my flesh" is more or less equivalent to "This is my body, which is given for you."

The promise of the Eucharist, then, already contained everything that would be realized in the institution. Thus we understand better why John did not regard it as necessary to repeat the account of the institution, which Christians constantly heard in the liturgy. A second observation is of no less importance: John's Gospel transmits to us key actions and words of the Last Supper. It recounts the washing of the feet and the words spoken by Jesus by way of commentary on the Eucharistic meal. Taking his starting point in the Eucharist, the Master expounds, more amply than he had before, the most essential points of his doctrine, such as the new commandment of love. The prayer with which this teaching closes sheds light on the thrust of the offering and thanksgiving that characterize the Eucharist (John 17:1–26).

Indeed, John is the Evangelist who best shows us the Eucharist as a mystery of the divine eternity permeating the human condition. As early as the Prologue of his Gospel, he had presented the Word made flesh. This flesh, assumed for a human life like our own, is the flesh given in the food of the Eucharist. In the discourse of interpretation of the multiplication of the loaves, John emphasizes the eternity of the life communicated by the Eucharist. After all, the one who eats the flesh of the Son of Man and drinks his blood "has eternal life" (see John 6:54). It is a matter of flesh in its glorious state, flesh that is given life by the Spirit. Beyond any doubt, the communication of divine life demonstrates the grandeur of the Eucharist: the eternity belonging to the Son of Man penetrates human hearts.

This does not mean that the Evangelist forgets the intrinsic value of human life. The Son of Man is a divine personage who has taken human nature, and the Eucharistic flesh, while animated by the life-giving Spirit, remains a flesh that is authentically human. The historical deed of the institution is not absolutely overshadowed: John's Gospel is the one that gives us the most complete experience of what occurred at the Last Supper. It furnishes us with a better grasp of the sentiments of Christ at the moment of the institution of the Eucharist.

In the drama of Judas's betrayal, it is John who reveals to us how wounded Jesus was by that disloyalty, a disloyalty consummated in the moment of the Eucharistic meal. In the dialogue between Jesus and the disciples, we observe that the Eucharist had transmitted the most intense relations of intimacy and serene trust.

We have need of a historical confirmation of the institution of the Eucharist, but we also have need of going as deeply as possible into the mystery. John helps us to do so.

Passover Climate of the Institution

The institution of the Eucharist took place in a Passover perspective, since it is accomplished before the Jewish festival of Passover. There has been discussion, however, on the nature of the meal taken by Jesus with the disciples. Was it an actual Passover supper? The difficulty flows from the divergence in chronology between Saint John and the Synoptics. For the Synoptics, Jesus died on the feast of Passover, while for John he died on the eve of that celebration. But if he died on the eve, then the meal taken by him with the disciples seems not to have been a Passover supper, since it would have taken place two days before the feast, the evening preceding his condemnation to the Cross. And so the question arises: Will we be able to assert only a Passover climate at the Last Supper, or should it be seen as a Passover supper? How can we solve the chronological problem posed by the divergence between John and the Synoptics?

Before we examine the problem of the exact date of Jesus' death, let us notice that the Gospel testimony seems not to have left any doubt about the Passover character of the Last Supper. "On the first day of Unleavened Bread, when the Passover lamb is sacrificed, his disciples said to him, 'Where do you want us to go and make the preparations for you to eat the Passover?'" (Mark 14:14).

Matthew stresses that the Master's directives were faithfully executed: "The disciples did as Jesus had directed them, and they prepared the Passover meal" (Matt. 26:19). Not only does the word "Passover" indicate beyond any doubt the Passover supper, but the particular care with which Jesus gave his instructions for the preparation confirms the Passover nature of the meal. The disciples' fidelity in following the orders they have received, a fidelity expressly recorded, is confirmation of this.

No less characteristic is Luke's sentence, "I have eagerly desired to eat this Passover with you before I suffer" (Luke 22:15–16). The fact that he ate the Passover meal, then, is of evident importance. Besides, in subjoining (literally), "until it is fulfilled," Jesus conveys that the Passover meal, in its basic significance, will now receive a new reality, one bearing on the Reign.

Further: a series of indicators can be identified that harmonize with the proper characteristics of the Passover supper, as, for example, the allusion to the ritual purity required for that meal (see John 13:10) or the conclusion of the supper with the last part of the hymn of the Hallel. A convergence of details strengthens the more explicit declarations of the Gospels. Not by chance, then, did Ephrem the Syrian, in the fourth century, alluding to the night of Jesus' Passover supper, intone this beatitude: "Blessed are you, O last night of all, as in you has been accomplished the night of Egypt. On you has our Lord eaten the little Passover, and himself become the great Passover.... Behold the Passover that passes, and the Passover that passes not. Behold the figure, and behold its fulfillment."[4]

---

4. "Hymn on the Crucifixion," 3, 2, ed. Lamy, 656.

Chapter 3

The Eucharist:
Name and Nature

Plurality of Names

Many names have been given the sacrament instituted by Jesus at the Last Supper. The Eucharist presents a multitude of aspects and therefore has been designated by many names.

In the primitive Church, it was called "the breaking of the bread." The breaking of the bread was reserved to the person seated at the head of the table; it acquired a new meaning at the Passover meal at which the body of Christ was given as food. In their encounter with the risen Christ at Emmaus, the disciples recognized the Master in the breaking of the bread (Luke 24:35). Even if it was a matter only of a prelude to the meal, because of Jesus' disappearance, the Evangelist Luke sees here the sign that henceforward his presence will be offered in the Eucharist. In the Acts of the Apostles, among the distinctive traits of the first community he cites the breaking of the bread, specifying that it was celebrated every day in homes (Acts 2:42–47).

The later term "Eucharist" was adopted in reference to the prayer of thanksgiving pronounced by Jesus for the consecration of the bread and wine. "Give thanks" in Greek was *eucharistein*. This prayer had given the meal a new meaning and value, based essentially on the relationship of Jesus with the Father. Jesus' prayer was regarded as so significant that the term *Eucharistia* came to indicate the rite or celebration in its entirety. John Chrysostom, for his part, explains that the reason why the holy mysteries are called the "Eucharist" ("Thanksgiving") "is that they are the record of many benefits, and show us the fundamental plane of God's salvation, disposing us ever to return thanks. . . . The priest, therefore, when he offers the divine sacrifice, commands us to return thanks for the entire world, for those who have already lived and for those

51

who live now, for those who have already been born and for those who will be born."[5]

Among the other names is that of "Supper," to be explained of course by the fact that the Eucharist was celebrated at that Last Supper on which it conferred a definitive character.

In parallel, we have the "Lord's Supper," that is, the meal bequeathed by the Lord Jesus to his disciples.

The term *synaxis*, "gathering," refers to the assembly convoked for the Eucharistic celebration. It suggests the ideal oneness of the community, a unity realized in the Eucharist.

"Memorial" signifies that which was instituted in memory of Christ — more precisely, that which renders his passion and resurrection present in the life of the Church.

The expressions "Holy Liturgy" and "Holy Mysteries" have been used for the Eucharist, even though as such they have a more general meaning. They denote in the case of the Eucharist the liturgical celebration par excellence, the most complete expression of the mystery of salvation.

"Holy Sacrament" indicates more particularly the body and blood of Christ made present in the celebration.

"Holy Sacrifice" expresses more particularly the gift that renews for the Church the sacrificial offering of the cross.

"Communion" is widely used to mean participation in the Eucharistic meal. Saint Paul himself spoke of a sharing (in Latin, *communio*) in the blood of Christ and in the body of Christ, and placed the accent on the effect of this communion not only in uniting persons to Christ, but in uniting in one body those who partake of it (1 Cor. 10:16–17). "Communion," then, has a twin meaning: union with Christ, and the concrete principle of the union of the faithful with one another.

The presence of the body of Christ under the sign of bread is declared in many formulae: "Bread from Heaven," "Bread of Angels," "Supersubstantial Bread," *Viaticum* (Lat., bread for a journey).

The most common term, "Mass," or "Holy Mass," comes from

5. *Homily on the Gospel of Matthew*, 25:3, PG 57:331.

the formula with which the faithful are dismissed at the end of the celebration ("Ite, missa est").

The Name "Eucharist" Prevails

Evolution of the Terminology

The Gospel texts enable us to understand the terminological evolution that led to the formation of the term "Eucharist" for the prayer Jesus offered during the Last Supper, and finally the entire sequence of the rite instituted by him.

In the accounts of Mark (14:22) and Matthew (26:26), Jesus' prayer at the consecration of the bread is recorded as a prayer of blessing. The participle used in the text (*eulogēsas*) means literally, "Having blessed." Taking up the bread, Jesus pronounces the blessing, according to Jewish custom.

In order to specify the sense of this prayer, we have to say that it is not so much a blessing *of* the bread as it is a blessing *over* the bread. In the religious vocabulary of the Jews, a "blessing" meant, on the one hand, the benevolence with which God lavished benefits on the people, and on the other hand the homage of the people who blessed God for so much that they had received. The prayer before and after a meal consisted in a blessing.[6]

We find an example in the account of the multiplication of the loaves. "Taking the five loaves and the two fish, he looked up to heaven, and blessed and broke the loaves" (Mark 6:41; cf. 14:19, Luke 9:16). Since the multiplication of the loaves is the miracle that presages the Eucharist, the prayer that precedes the miracle is reported to us as a prelude to the one that preceded the institution of the Eucharist. It is a blessing, a *eulogia*, and is not yet called the "Eucharist."

We could have thought, then, that the prayer pronounced at the Last Supper was likewise a *eulogia*, or blessing, pronounced according to Jewish usage. Furthermore, this expectation could have justified the fact that Jesus had selected as the cup of his blood the third cup of the Passover meal, called the "cup of blessing." Saint Paul expressly alludes to it: "The cup of blessing that we

---

6. See Joachim Jeremias, *Le parole dell'Ultima Cena* (Brescia: Paideia, 1973).

bless, is it not a sharing in the blood of Christ?" (1 Cor. 10:16). That cup could have left its name to the rite of Communion in the blood of Christ, conferring upon it the appellation of "blessing," or *eulogia.*

It would seem that Mark and Matthew wished to introduce precisely this appellation in their version of Jesus' prayer of the consecration of the bread. Nevertheless, not even these two Evangelists stopped at an interpretation of the prayer in question in terms of *eulogia.* They refer to the prayer of the consecration of the cup as a "Eucharistic" prayer: "After giving thanks..." (*eucharistēsas:* Mark 14:23, Matt. 26:27).

And so we have a transition from *eulogia* to *eucharistia,* "Eucharist." Paul, although he is speaking of the cup of blessing, uses solely the verb "to give thanks" (*eucharistein*) to define Jesus' prayer in the account of the institution of the sacrament (1 Cor. 11:24). Luke does the same (22:17).

We observe, then, that dating from the first testimonials on the institution, notwithstanding a starting point in the Jewish prayer of blessing, Jesus' prayer at the Last Supper receives a new designation, one that confers on it a specific character and no longer permits assimilation to the Jewish liturgy. The designation in question is that of "Eucharist."

After the Gospels, the writing called the *Didachē* or "Teaching of the Twelve Apostles" denotes as the "Eucharist" not only the prayer of thanksgiving pronounced by Jesus, but the rite in its entirety: "On the Lord's own day, assemble in common to break bread and offer thanks; but first confess your sins, so that your sacrifice may be pure."[7] Still later, Saint Justin preserves only the verb *eucharistein,* in reporting the tradition of the Gospels on Jesus' command given to his disciples at the Last Supper:

> Not as ordinary bread or as ordinary drink do we partake of them, but just as, through the word of God, our Savior Jesus Christ became Incarnate and took upon himself flesh and blood for our salvation, so, we have been taught, the food which has been made the Eucharist by the prayer of his

---

7. *The Teaching of the Twelve Apostles,* no. 14; trans. James A. Kleist (Westminster, Md.: Newman, 1948), 23.

word...is both the flesh and blood of that Jesus who was made flesh.[8]

Thus, more exactly, the Eucharist means the transformation occurring in the bread and wine. The thanksgiving is regarded as an efficacious petition, owing to the bread and wine becoming the flesh and blood of Christ.

Novelty of the Thanksgiving

In using the term "thanksgiving" to describe Jesus' prayer at the Last Supper, Christians wished to underscore the novelty demonstrated, which was of a marvelous efficacy. No Jewish "blessing" had had so wondrous an efficacy. The bread and wine that have become the body and blood of Christ testify to the transformative power of his prayer and his words.

The novelty did not consist only in this efficacy, however. It was expressed through a specific attitude, that of thanksgiving, which was not equivalent to a blessing. While ancient Hebrew had no proper term for the sense of gratitude,[9] Jesus' prayer accentuates this sense.

The Jews' prayer of blessing implied an attitude of praise, of which the Psalms convey to us some remarkable expressions. Praise celebrates the marvels of God, exalting them precisely in a sense of the human being's feeling infinitely surpassed by the divine transcendence and omnipotence. The greater the distance appearing between God and creation, the more ardent the expressions of praise lifted up to that divine transcendence.

Thanksgiving tends to acknowledge the greatness of the divine miracles, then, but the emphasis is especially on what human neediness receives from these marvels. Although the distance between Creator and creatures is stressed, thanksgiving seeks to express admiration for the communication of the divine riches to creatures. It desires to render homage to God for such generosity by returning thanks. Not that there is no consciousness of the divine

---

8. Justin, *Apology*, 66, 2; trans. Thomas B. Falls (Washington, D.C.: Catholic University of America Press, 1948), 105–6.

9. See C. Giraudo, *La struttura letteraria della preghiera eucharistica* (Rome: Pontifical Biblical Institute, 1981), 264.

transcendence; only, thanksgiving emphasizes astonishment at the condescension of that transcendence toward the world, in order to pour forth its benefits there.

Thanksgiving develops when God approaches the human being in order to strike a covenant or communion with that individual. The ancient covenant itself contained an invitation to acknowledge the divine goodness being manifested in a special way in behalf of the chosen people. But the accent was usually on the fearsome aspect of God's sovereignty, so discordant with the sinfulness of the people. In the new covenant, the outlook for human destiny has been profoundly changed by the total, definitive openness of God's love for humanity. The sovereign deed with which the Father bestows his Son cannot arouse fear and cannot be received with praise alone. It must call forth thanksgiving.

This thanksgiving receives its primordial and most perfect expression from Christ himself. On one side, Jesus acknowledged the gift conferred by the Father on humanity in all of its importance and value: he speaks frequently of the Father, precisely in order to have the divine solicitude appreciated, a solicitude of numerous manifestations of God's goodness. He desires to communicate to his disciples his own admiration and gratitude for all that he receives from the Father. He lives in thanksgiving and influences his disciples to do the same.

At the same time, in the impulse of gratitude that lifts him up to the Father, Jesus aspires to a response to the Father's love in the fullness of his filial love. "Thanks" tends to restore to the one who lavishes gifts on us something of what we have received. As incarnate Son of God, only Jesus can restore to the Father all that he receives from him and present that person with a love just as intense as that of which he himself is the object. While for all other human beings the homage of gratitude necessarily remains limited, far inferior to what has been received, the Son is in a position to return to the Father all that he has received, in its integrity. To the total gift of the Father, the total gift of the Son responds.

This is why Jesus, in thanksgiving, addresses to the Father an offering that commits his whole person. The prayer of thanksgiving confers on the offering its full value. All that has been received from the Father is restored to the Father through an integral offering.

Thanksgiving in Jesus' Life

Preparation for the Eucharist

Jesus' intimate attitude of gratitude was not improvised by him at the moment of the Last Supper, finally to be expressed in the prayer preceding the consecration of the bread and wine. It was a special disposition of Jesus' filial attitude. It had been developed and manifested throughout the course of his public life, as he went about fulfilling his mission.

Hymn of Jubilee. The Hymn of Jubilee is contained in the explosion of enthusiasm with which Jesus sought to pay homage to the Father for the revelation reserved to the little ones: "Jesus rejoiced in the Holy Spirit and said, 'I thank you, Father, Lord of heaven and earth, because you have hidden these things from the wise and the intelligent and have revealed them to infants; yes, Father, for such was your gracious will' " (Luke 10:21).

In Jesus, gratitude is not a sentiment of acknowledgment rising simply from a human being to God. It wells up from the divine person of the Son, who, in his earthly existence, turns to the Father.

This is the reason why, among Christians, thanksgiving will not be simply a motion of human nature, but will have to be inspired by the Holy Spirit, who gives believers a share in the Son's own impulse of gratitude, and who carries their homage to the Father's throne on high.

Raising of Lazarus. The raising of Lazarus is the occasion of a prayer of thanksgiving on Jesus' part that confirms the importance of this disposition in Jesus' interior life: "Father, I thank you for having heard me" (John 11:41).

We are astonished that this prayer was made even before the miracle had occurred. One would say that Jesus' thanksgiving had the aim of provoking the miracle, as it would later have in the case of the numberless miracles that would take place by the power of the Eucharist.

In reporting Jesus' words, Saint John's Gospel has sought to clarify their meaning in order to respond to the difficulty that they could occasion: Would it have been possible for Jesus not to be heard in his prayer to the Father? "I knew that you always hear me, but have said this for the sake of the crowd standing here, so that they may believe that you sent me" (John 11:42). Precisely because he is sure of being heard, Jesus pronounces his thanksgiving before working, with the words of consecration, the miracle represented by the presence of his body and blood.

He wishes the crowd to hear his prayer of thanksgiving before the raising of Lazarus, because this will be the greatest and most impressive miracle of his public life, the miracle that announces his own resurrection in the most suggestive manner. Before working the miracle and ordering Lazarus to emerge from the tomb, he wishes to have it understood that he is not limiting himself to acting on his own authority. He has implored the Father to grant him the strength to work this miracle, and this is why he addresses to him his prayer of thanksgiving. By shedding light on this relationship with the Father, he shows that, just as is verified for the greatest of miracles, so also does it occur with all of the others: all derive from a sovereign deed of the Father; all of them are received from him.

Besides, it seems that, in this thanksgiving for the raising of Lazarus, in a certain manner Jesus' thanksgiving for his own resurrection was anticipated. This was a gratitude that will not be able to be pronounced on earth, because the risen Christ will be in the state of heavenly life. Just as Lazarus's resurrection prefigured that of the Savior, so the act of thanksgiving pronounced at Lazarus's tomb referred to the miracle that crowned the drama of redemption.

At the Moment of the Institution

The manifestations of gratitude before the Last Supper are a help to us in understanding the depth of Jesus' sense, and expression, of thanksgiving at the moment of the institution of the Eucharist.

The words that record it are very brief and could seem banal or routine: "After giving thanks...." Their repetition in the Eucharistic celebration may sometimes pass unobserved. But the prayer addressed at that moment by Christ to the Father is animated by the entire thrust of the thanksgiving that had matured in Jesus' soul.

The brevity of the report must be completed by indications left to us by John's Gospel on the Last Supper and by certain words of Jesus that shed light on the meaning of the Eucharist.

Even though he does not report the institution of the Eucharist, which we find in the other Evangelists and in Saint Paul, John the Evangelist introduces us as profoundly as possible into Jesus' state of mind at the moment of the Supper. "Jesus knew that his hour had come to depart from this world and go to the Father. Having loved his own who were in the world, he loved them to the end" (John 13:1). He knew of Judas's project of betrayal, but he was conscious of a far more important truth: he knew that "the Father had given all things into his hands, and that he had come from God and was going to God" (John 13:3).

This awareness of having received everything from the Father is essential in Jesus' thanksgiving. In order to thank the Father with all of the sincerity of our hearts, we must know what the Father has given us. We can appreciate the divine gift only insofar as we observe it in our lives. Jesus knew all of the power of which he disposed. He acknowledged that he had come from the Father. The Father had placed everything in his hands, and so his gratitude rose to the Father. As Son, he had received all that the Father possessed: the Father's generosity had been manifested without the slightest reserve.

Jesus knew besides that he had come from the Father and was returning to that Father. At the end of the discourse held during the Supper, he clearly asserts: "I came from the Father and have come into the world; again, I am leaving the world and am going to the Father" (John 16:28). This consciousness of returning to the Father and this will to do so constitute an essential aspect of thanksgiving as it is expressed in the Eucharist. Returning to the Father, the Son can restore to that Father everything that he has received.

Given this return, Jesus can express his gratitude under the form of a total offering. As the Son, who has a relationship of equality with the Father, with his offering he can restore to the Father all that the Father has bestowed upon him. He is the only person capable of an act of thanksgiving to God in which the offering is not inferior to the fullness received.

In this offering, he commits a love without limit, a love that reaches its extreme development in sacrifice. It is the offering that enables Jesus, in the Eucharist, to give the gift of his own flesh and blood, to make himself present once more among human beings. This offering belongs to the nature of the Eucharistic thanksgiving in a real manner. We should fall far short of the truth were we to conceive of Jesus' thanksgiving only as the expression of a sentiment of gratitude. We can understand why the Council of Trent condemns any definition of the sacrifice of the Mass only as a sacrifice of praise and gratitude, or as a simple commemoration of the sacrifice of the Cross, without any propitiatory value. We must conceive of Christ's thanksgiving in the fullness of meaning and value it took on with his sacrifice. It is the response to the Father's gift, which consists in a propitiatory gift that obtains reconciliation between God and a sinful humanity.

Thus, this thanksgiving includes a maximal generosity, through the commitment of the Savior in the redemptive offering. All that the Father has bestowed on the Son in the Incarnation has as its objective the work of salvation. All that the Son offers in response to the Father is intended as accomplishment of his mission. His thanksgiving derives from the Father's primordial gift and realizes the course of the offering that ascends to God.

Intensity of the Son's Movement to the Father

Jesus' prayer of thanksgiving, on the occasion of the institution of the Eucharist, was the ultimate expression of his interior disposition, developed throughout his earthly life. It expresses his consciousness of having received all from the Father, and his will to return to that Father through the offering of his sacrifice.

It was not only the expression of a sense of gratitude. It issued from the filial soul of Jesus, ready to give the absolute gift of self, in response to the total gift of the Father, who had entrusted all things to the hands of the only-begotten Son.

This was expressed by the power of that thanksgiving, totally inserted as it was into the drama of redemption, and of a value or degree that enabled it to ensure full efficacy to the sacrifice. All of the intensity of the Son's thrust and movement toward the Father, which had developed during Jesus' earthly existence, was manifested, giving a higher sense to the offering of the bread and wine, which became an offering of his body and blood.

This filial impulse, this thanksgiving, had its origin in the eternal mystery of the Trinity, according to Saint John's declaration: "In the beginning was the Word, and the Word was with God" (John 1:1). From all eternity, the Son was with the Father, in a permanent, inexhaustible dynamism. It was this dynamism of the Son, who was attached to the Father, that dominated the route of the Incarnation and that aroused in Jesus' human soul the motion of thanksgiving. In that thanksgiving, all of the strength of a divine dynamism was committed. The Eucharistic prayer welled up from the love of the Son for the Father.

Not without reason, then, in the institution of the new Supper, Christians recognized the essential importance of thanksgiving and called the meal offered by Christ to his disciples the Eucharist. They saw, in the impulse of the Son's thanksgiving to the Father, the secret power that transformed the bread and wine into the Savior's body and blood.

Role of the Holy Spirit in Jesus' Thanksgiving

We must recognize, in Jesus' thanksgiving, not only the power of the divine person of the Son of God who was ascending to the Father, but the presence of the Holy Spirit, as well.

As we have seen, it is this presence that is especially featured in the Gospel of Luke (Luke 10:21), when that Evangelist reports the Hymn of Jubilee. Jesus experiences a transport of joy in the Holy Spirit. While the Gospel of Matthew (11:25) limits itself to reporting to us the words with which Jesus praises and thanks the Father for the benevolence manifested with regard to the least ones, Luke seeks to draw our attention especially to the Master's interior dispositions — to the enthusiasm that sustains his prayer to the Father and, especially, to the Holy Spirit, who arouses this enthusiasm.

In particular, Luke is the Evangelist who has insisted the most on the role of the Holy Spirit throughout Jesus' earthly life. In the thanksgiving, this role is not to be explained only by the fact that Spirit means breath and inspires dispositions of enthusiasm. More profoundly, the Holy Spirit is the divine person who unites the Son to the Father. The Holy Spirit animates the filial thrust with which the incarnate Son pays the Father the homage of the Son's person.

Let us also recall how the Letter to the Hebrews underscores the Trinitarian aspect of the redemptive sacrifice. "Christ... through the eternal Spirit offered himself without blemish to God" (Heb. 9:14). The offering of the Son on the Cross is carried to the Father by the Spirit. This Spirit is called eternal by reason of the "eternal redemption" the Spirit works.

In other words, in the offering as in the thanksgiving, the route that goes from the Son to the Father passes by way of the Holy Spirit. Indeed, as we have emphasized above apropos of Jesus' thanksgiving at the Last Supper, this thanksgiving implies offering and is expressed in the offering of the redemptive sacrifice, by way of an integral return to the Father. We understand, then, the essential role performed by the Holy Spirit in the Eucharistic mystery: the Spirit guarantees the fulfillment of the offering in thanksgiving.

Thanksgiving in Christian Life

Influence on All of Christian Life

If we must acknowledge in the Eucharist the decisive influence of Jesus' thanksgiving, then all of Christian life should be orientated in this direction. Beyond a doubt, Christ's intention was to develop in his Church a climate of thanksgiving. The Eucharistic celebration should foster dispositions of gratitude in those who participate in it. And, the celebration aside, an effort to stimulate those thoughts, sentiments, and attitudes characteristic of thanksgiving is required.

The "Eucharist" should not be a mere name, the name of a sacrament. It should be a reality realized in all aspects of existence and behavior. It is the reality that took form in Jesus and that ought to be the model for thinking and living for those who believe in him.

The Spirit and an Enduring Attitude of Thanksgiving

Relationships between God and humanity have need of a spirit of thanksgiving in order to develop harmoniously. At the moment in which Jesus was caught up in the most difficult of his trials, which must have made him feel all of the pain of an unjust condemnation as well as the humiliations and sufferings of the torment of the Cross, he sought to accord full value to thanksgiving. Instead of accusing the Father, who had sent him this trial, he expressly thanked him for all that he had received and was receiving from God. Through the institution of the Eucharist, he wished to share with all human beings the homage with which he acknowledged all that he had received and wished to attract their attention to the immense, sovereign goodness that guided the destiny of the universe.

In his far-sightedness, without a doubt Jesus was altogether correct to point to thanksgiving as the means to guide humanity along that route. His example encourages all of those who are overwhelmed with trial to lift their gaze on high to discover in the Father the one who deserves to be thanked for so many benefits. The Christ of the Last Supper helps believers to discover a divine benevolence that ceaselessly lavishes its gifts on human beings, gifts too frequently ignored and little appreciated. A "eucharistic" view develops.

This view, this regard, entails at the same time a deliverance. It delivers the human spirit from the obsession that can register every sort of evil. It does not allow the heart to become imprisoned or paralyzed by the forces of evil manifested in social relations. The view of all that occurs in the world could lead to pessimism and destroy an outlook of the victorious power of the work of redemption.

Only a regard of gratitude enables us to discover the immensity of the divine love that conquers all of the forces of evil. Here is a wellspring of sound optimism, which avoids judgments too inclined to condemnation and, by showing the higher goodness of heaven, enables us better to discern the encouraging aspects of human behaviors. It is the source of true hope, a hope that has its foundation in the essentially salvific intent of the Father and in the implementation of all means to realize that intention.

Christ, who had this regard of thanksgiving at the moment he faced the redemptive drama, communicates it to human beings at every moment, but especially in the hour of suffering. Through the celebration of the Eucharist, he seeks to diffuse his regard throughout humanity by sending it his witness. The disciples are witnesses of his thanksgiving, that is, witnesses of a love recognizable through the generosity of his gifts and in the offering that such a generosity arouses.

Chapter 4

Jesus Really Present, according to His Words

What distinguishes the Eucharist from the other sacraments is that in the Eucharist, Christ himself is present with his body and his blood. The effect of the words of consecration is not simply to communicate a particular grace, but to render present the one in whom all grace has its origin.

Reality of the Body and Blood

Through the reality of the body and blood of Christ, a body and blood offered as food and drink, the Eucharist presents itself as a mystery transcending all sensory evidence. The proposition of the presence of Christ's body and blood, where those who share in the celebration can see only the bread and wine, can be accepted only through an allegiance of faith. The Eucharist imposes the necessity of believing what is not seen. However, such a necessity inevitably raises questions and requires a clearer indication of the reasons for believing. It is a matter especially of clarifying the sense and foundation of what has come to be defined as the real presence: this sense and this foundation have been the object of continuous reflection in the development of the doctrine of the Church.

In this reflection, we must never forget the starting point, the words pronounced by Jesus. We have already cited the testimonials of Paul and the Gospels, which have transmitted these words to us. Now it is a matter of studying their meaning more in depth, in order to verify the reality of the body and blood of the Savior as it is formulated by Christ himself.

Affirmation of the Reality

Probably, taking the bread, Jesus said in Aramaic, "This, my flesh" — that is, "This is my flesh."

In the Aramaic language, the verb "to be" was omitted. However, that omission is far from attenuating the force of the assertion. The truth of the real presence does not depend on the use of the verb "to be." We may also observe that in other languages the words "Behold my flesh" do not include the verb "to be," and yet they signify the real presence of flesh.

In the Greek translation, which has sought faithfully to render the sense of the Aramaic formula, the verb "to be" is expressed: "This is my body." The Gospel accounts convey to us this translation, which was now included in the liturgical usage of Greek-speaking Christians. The Greek translation of the Aramaic leaves no doubt as to the real presence of the body of Christ.

Likewise, the formula used for the consecration of the wine includes the assertion of the reality of the blood. The assertion is evident in the Markan (12:42) and Matthean (26:28) versions: "This is my blood of the covenant." It is evident in Paul's version, as well (1 Cor. 11:25: "This cup is the new covenant in my blood"), and in Luke's version (22:20), although the latter lacks the verb "to be." The presence of the blood of Christ is indicated as the content of the cup, rendering the latter a sign of covenant in the sacrifice.

"My Flesh"

Following the indications of the Gospel accounts, we could have thought that Jesus used the term "body" and not "flesh." Indeed these accounts report the formula, "This is my body." What we have, however, is a Greek translation, and the problem is to know what Aramaic term was used by Jesus.

There is every indication that Jesus used the term "flesh." Indeed, "flesh" is the Semitic term used in parallel with "blood." We always find in the Bible the pair "flesh and blood" and never "body and blood." Jesus himself uses the expression "flesh and blood" to indicate the human as opposed to what is revealed by the Father (Matt. 16:17).

John's Gospel confirms this use of the term "flesh" in a Eucharistic context. It reports the basic declaration according to which flesh and blood are indissolubly joined: "Very truly, I tell you, unless you eat the flesh of the Son of Man and drink his blood, you have no life in you" (John 6:53). The expression "the flesh of the Son of Man" has a particular Semitic flavor that harks back more clearly to Jesus' language, given that Jesus was accustomed to designate himself as the Son of Man when he wished to express his divine origin and his mission. Speaking of the flesh of the Son of Man, he sought to convey that his body was not given as food as the body of an ordinary human being living on earth could have been: his flesh could be given as food only by virtue of the glorious lot assigned to the Son of Man. Later, in order to clarify the sense of the Eucharistic proclamation, he will define his flesh as the flesh of the Son of Man restored to heavenly glory through the Ascension (John 6:62).

This flesh of the Son of Man is none other than the flesh of Jesus, so that the very assertion of his power to give his life is expressed through the words "my flesh": "Those who eat my flesh and drink my blood have eternal life, and I will raise them up on the last day" (John 6:54).

The declaration is very akin to the accounts of the institution of the Eucharist: "Eat my flesh" and "Drink my blood" correspond to the words "Eat: this is my body; drink: this is my blood," with the difference that the term used is "flesh" (in Greek, *sarx*) and not "body" (*sōma*). We believe that the author of the Gospel, here recounting the institution that he had not included in his account of the Last Supper, attributes to Jesus the following words: "Eat: this [is] my flesh," and, "Drink: this [is] my blood."

The expression "my flesh" is emphatically used in Christ's justification of the invitation to eat and drink: "For my flesh is true food and my blood is true drink" (John 6:55). This better explains why Jesus does not speak of bread or wine. All of the reality of the nourishment is found in his flesh, and all of the reality of the drink is found in his blood.

This use of the term "flesh" in the formula of the consecration is also implicit in the declaration "The bread that I will give for the life of the world is my flesh" (John 6:51). The word "bread" is pronounced, but certainly not in the ordinary sense of the term, nor is it used to designate the material bread that serves as a sign in the Eucharistic celebration. It is a matter of the "living bread that came down from heaven" (John 6:51), which is Jesus himself. "Bread" is used as a synonym for "nourishment."

The assertion "is my flesh" not only confirms the supposition that Jesus expressed himself in this way at the Last Supper but also indicates the formula in its most complete version: "for the life of the world... my flesh" indicates the flesh given or offered for the salvation of humanity, or else, in parallel with what is said of the blood "poured out for many," the flesh sacrificed for many, for the human multitude. The indication of this purpose is essential: Christ's flesh is given as food in virtue of the sacrifice offered for the world.

Wealth of the Meaning of the Term "Flesh"

The words "Take, eat; this is my body" correctly translate the Aramaic words used by Jesus. Indeed, what we have, essentially, is an assertion of the reality of Jesus' body, with the invitation to take it as nourishment. Still, it is interesting to emphasize what flesh meant in the Semitic mentality. The fact that Jesus had said "my flesh" sheds a particular light on the gift he was making of himself in the Eucharistic meal.

Not inappropriately, Christian piety has expressed, in the poetry of a famous hymn, the "true body" born of the Virgin Mary:

Ave, verum Corpus, natum ex Maria Virgine,
Vere passum, immolatum in cruce pro homine,
Cujus latus perforatum aqua fluxit et sanguine.
Esto nobis praegustatum mortis in examine,
O Jesu dulcis, O Jesu pie, O Jesu fili Mariae.

Hail, true body, born of the Virgin Mary,
who have truly suffered and been immolated on the Cross
    for us,
whose pierced side flowed with water and blood!
May we have received it in the hour of death,
O sweet Jesus, O loving Jesus, O Jesus, Son of Mary!

The flesh offered at the Last Supper, and immolated on the Cross was the same flesh as Jesus had received from his mother. In saying "My flesh," he was conscious of returning to humanity that which the Blessed Virgin, owing to the wondrous intervention of the Holy Spirit, had given him in his birth. It is a flesh virginally conceived, and therefore of an exceptional value, that is given in the Eucharist.

We also gather its individual character. This is a flesh with a unique, absolutely pure origin, a flesh that came down from heaven to restore the flesh of all human beings. True, speaking of his flesh, Jesus was thinking of the human condition that he shared with all humanity. But as shown by the Virgin Birth, in Christ flesh takes on a new meaning. It is a flesh formed in an exceptional manner in order to inaugurate a new world of flesh.

Personal Presence

The term "flesh" does not have a meaning so circumscribed as to be limited only to the body properly so called. It often suggests the living being in its entirety, without any concern to make a distinction between the properties of the body and those of the soul. Hence it can be used to signify the whole person, although with the connotation of frailty.

To the flesh are attributed the most profound aspirations of the person. Desire of the flesh and desire of the soul are identified in the Psalms: "My soul faints for you; my flesh thirsts for you" (Ps. 63:1). The flesh cries out in joy at finding itself in God's dwelling: "My soul longs, indeed it faints, for the courts of the Lord; my heart and my flesh sing for joy to the living God" (Ps. 84:2). The biblical expression "all flesh" sometimes stood for the whole of humanity: "All flesh had corrupted its ways upon the earth" (Gen. 6:12). All persons living on the earth are accused of perversion.

In saying, "This [is] my flesh," it seems that Jesus sought to express an involvement of his entire person, the gift that he was making of himself by giving his flesh as nourishment. True, this flesh regards a physical reality, but in the gift of this reality a gift is manifested that is more complete and more lofty, that of the person of the Son of God.

Meaningfully, in the words of the discourse of the proclamation of the Eucharist, we find, as equivalent expressions: "Those who eat my flesh and drink my blood..." (John 6:54) and "Whoever eats me..." (6:57). To eat the flesh of Christ is to eat Christ himself, precisely because the gift of his body involves the gift of his person. His "flesh," then, must not be understood as simple bodily reality detached from the soul and the person. Christ's person becomes food, and this implies on his part the gift of his entire self. Jesus did not hesitate to say, "Whoever eats me," thus showing forth the point to which he is taking his abasement and service, becoming the nourishment of those to whom he seeks to communicate his life.

When Jesus explains the nature of the meal that he wishes to offer to humanity, he vigorously asserts this personal presence. With his emphatic assertion that henceforth persons are to eat the flesh of the Son of Man and drink his blood, he presents himself, in his person, as the food that gives life.

He calls himself bread from heaven, "bread of God," and the "bread which comes down from heaven and gives life to the world" (John 6:33). His discourse had begun with the declaration that it is the "Son of Man" who bestows the "food that endures for eternal life" (John 6:27). But this gift of food coincides with the gift of the person, because it is the bread given by the Father, and this bread is the Son himself, the essential gift given by the Father to humanity. Jesus is the bread come down from heaven: he is the one who, through the Eucharist, gives life to the world.

The statement "I am the bread of life" (John 6:35, 48) is very significant. It stresses the truth that Jesus not only gives the bread of eternal life, but that this bread is himself. In the context, which recalls the bread from heaven given by Moses to the people in the wilderness, Jesus wishes to emphasize that he, in his person, realizes what the manna of the Old Testament has prefigured. The manna was but a prefiguration: it was not really the bread from heaven, as is expressly stated: "I tell you, it was not Moses who gave you the bread from heaven, but it is my Father who gives you the true bread from heaven" (John 6:32). All of the reality of the bread from heaven is found in Jesus. It is he who fulfills in his person what had been proclaimed in prefiguration by the manna.

The accent placed on the identity of the Eucharistic nourishment with Jesus' person is all the more vigorous in that the expression "I am" is the characteristic formula with which Jesus gives his audience to understand that his very name is that of God, and that his being is absolute being. He defines a fundamental property of this being: the bread of life, that is, nourishment that secures the divine life.

The insistence of the Gospel of John on the bread given as food does not interfere with a more attentive consideration of the divine being involved in the gift of Jesus' flesh. The primordial element in the Eucharist is the involvement of the person of the Son. The declaration "I am" (*egō eimi*) precedes the affirmation "This [is] my flesh" and clarifies all of its value.

It is specifically Jesus' flesh that is given as food, but in the gift of his flesh the gift of the person of Christ is manifested. Thus, believers are invited to acknowledge, in the presence of Jesus' body, a personal presence. In his Semitic manner of speech, Jesus was using "my flesh" to speak of his whole person. In his consciousness of being the Son of the Father, he was considering his flesh as an exceptional property of his divine person.

In using the expression, "the flesh of the Son of Man" (John 6:53), Jesus was making a more intentional reference to the mystery of his person in the fulfillment of his mission. The bread of eternal life is given by the Son of Man, on whom "God the Father has set his seal" (John 6:27). The Father's seal is the Father's guarantee of the authenticity of Jesus' mission, a guarantee manifested in the episode of his baptism, with the descent of the Holy Spirit, and continuing to produce its effects through his miracles, signs of heavenly approval. This guarantee testifies that the Son of Man disposes of eternal life, and has the power to communicate it through the Eucharist.

In the assertion of the reality of the flesh offered as food, then, Christ's personal presence plays an essential role. It is the Son of God who is present in the flesh and who communicates to that flesh his nutritive power.

Eucharist and Trinity

Role and Presence of the Father

The teaching enunciated by Jesus in the discourse reported by Saint John does not limit itself to the assertion of Christ's personal presence. The Son is present in the Eucharist because the Father has sent him. The ultimate initiative of the gift of the Eucharist is that of the Father. True, the entire initiative of the work of salvation belongs to him: it is he who is at the origin of the redemptive Incarnation and its prolongation in the development of the Church. But the initiative of the Eucharistic meal must be attributed to him in an even more special manner, since, as Father, he has the task of feeding his children. The prayer to the Father that Jesus taught his disciples contains the request for daily bread.

It is the Father who gives food to humanity by giving his Son himself. Only he could give his Son, and in making this gift, he has given the most noble food that could have been given in answer to the spiritual needs of human life. In placing his flesh at the disposition of all in the Eucharistic meal, Jesus did not lose sight of the generous action of the Father. As in the whole fulfillment of his mission, he was aware of doing the work of the Father, in such an intimate union with that Father as to be able to say: "The Father who dwells in me does his works" (John 14:10).

Can we conclude from this that, in the Eucharist, besides the personal presence of Christ, we have an analogous presence of the Father? We must admit that, between the Son and the Father the most complete union exists: "The Father and I are one" (John 10:30), that is, one thing, one single being. They are inseparable. The Father must always be seen as the ultimate origin of the Eucharist.

Still, properly speaking, the personal presence expressed in the Eucharist is a particular presence of the person of the Son. When Jesus says, "this [is] my flesh," he is asserting that he is personally present in the body given as nourishment. It is his personal "I am," his divine person, that founds this presence of flesh. The words "my flesh" do not refer to the person of the Father, since the Father did not become incarnate and does not possess fleshly being.

In the utterly complete union characterizing the divine persons, there is a difference among those persons that renders the Father's activity singular: only the Son became incarnate. Even though the Incarnation was the work of the three divine persons, the person of the Son is the only one to have been made flesh, the only one who took on flesh as his property, his concrete attribute. This person, then, is the only one to have given his actual carnal presence.

In the Eucharist, as in the Incarnation, we must acknowledge the intervention of the three divine persons. But the proper action of the Son has the peculiarity of giving itself in his flesh. The personal presence communicated in the Eucharistic meal, then, is the presence of the incarnate Son.

The Father works in the sacrament, but not by the same title, since the Father has not assumed human flesh. His activity must be emphasized, as Jesus himself emphasizes it, declaring that it is the Father who "gives you the true bread from heaven" (John 6:32). Nevertheless, this action does not include for the Father a presence similar to that of the Son. During Christ's earthly life, only the person of the Son came into the world. Only the Son has had access, through the offering of his sacrifice, to a glorious state that, through his body, is manifested in the Resurrection and the Ascension. It is this glorious state that permits him to give himself, in this sacrament, to humanity, in order to nourish it with his own life. The Eucharistic presence, therefore, is a property of the person of the son.

To be sure, in the Eucharistic mystery the Trinity loses nothing of its oneness. The fact that the Eucharistic presence is exclusively that of the Son by no manner annuls the Son's perfect union with the Father, a union developed and declared in the very gift of the Eucharist. The Trinity is at work in all of the aspects of the mystery, but in such a way as to reinforce the presence of the person of Christ in his flesh, a presence with a specific character.

Role and Presence of the Holy Spirit

What we have said of the action of the Trinity in the Eucharistic mystery helps us in understanding the peculiar role of the Holy Spirit. We have already commented on the response given in view of the incomprehension of Jesus' audience, who had interpreted the invitation to eat the flesh of the Son of Man as if it had been a matter of a flesh given as nourishment in his earthly state. "It is the spirit that gives life" (John 6:63). Thus, Jesus stresses that the whole life-giving capacity of the Eucharist is due to the Holy Spirit. In the Eucharistic meal, he gives his flesh, but it is a flesh that has attained to the state of glory, where it is crowned by the Spirit. Without this contribution on the part of the Spirit, the flesh would have no power to communicate the spiritual life, eternal life. In itself, "the flesh is useless," as we read in the Johannine verse just cited. The *Apostolic Constitutions* — whose final redaction is from the end of the fourth century, but which contain a collection of much earlier material — effectively clarify the intimate relationship binding the Eucharist and the Holy Spirit. The epiclesis there recorded reads:

> We ask you to turn a benevolent regard upon these offerings presented to you — you, O God, who have need of nothing.... Send upon this sacrifice your Holy Spirit, witness of the sufferings of the Lord Jesus, that the Spirit may manifest in this bread the body of your Christ, and in this cup the blood of your Christ, in order that those who communicate may be confirmed in faith, may obtain the remission of their sins, may be delivered from the devil and from their error, may be filled with the Holy Spirit.[10]

The problem arises, then: Does the action of the Holy Spirit not involve a presence of the person of the Spirit that is associated to the presence of the person of Christ? Would such an association not lead us to see the Eucharist as a sacrament of the Holy Spirit and not only a sacrament of the person of the Savior? Could the two presences not appear, as it were, in competition, so that Eucharistic piety would point in two directions?

But we must point out a difference between the two presences. The properly Eucharistic presence remains basically the presence of Christ and, more precisely, of the Son in his human flesh. The Holy Spirit does not inaugurate a bond with flesh similar to that of the Incarnation. True, he effects the conception of the Son in the virginal womb of Mary, but he does not become flesh — unlike the Word, who does become flesh. Hence his presence in the Eucharist

---

10. *Constituzioni* 39, ed. Metzger, SC 336, 151–217.

is not of the same nature as that of Jesus. Jesus says, "This [is] my flesh," while the Holy Spirit could not say this.

The Holy Spirit intervenes in the realization of these words. By way of the Holy Spirit, Jesus, in the Eucharistic celebration, renders his body and blood present. It is the Spirit who fills Jesus' flesh with divine life and divine power and who thus contributes, in a sovereign manner, to the efficacy of the Eucharist. But while entirely animated by the Spirit, this flesh remains the flesh of Christ. The Holy Spirit guarantees the reality and value of a divine presence that, nevertheless, is that of the incarnate Son.

The conjunction of Jesus' two declarations expresses the specific character of his Eucharistic presence: "I am," and "This [is] my flesh." The assertion "I am" would not suffice if we removed it from its context of human life, since this assertion is limited to an affirmation of the identity of his divine person, an identity verified also in the Father and the Spirit, and an identity of the single divine essence and being, God. The "I am" is an expression of the exclusive identity of Jesus, although with the indirect implication of the assertion "This [is] my flesh." It is his personal possession of flesh that, in the work of salvation, distinguishes the Son from the other two persons.

In particular, flesh distinguishes the Son from the Spirit. The opposition between flesh and spirit is set forth by Saint Paul, who has seen there a struggle between the strength of sin and the power of the Holy Spirit (see Gal. 4:21–31, Rom. 7:17–18, 8:9–10). This pejorative conceptualization of flesh is overcome in the Eucharistic formula employed by Jesus. In saying "This [is] my flesh," he was, in some sort, sealing the reconciliation of flesh and spirit. He was expressing his personal presence, a presence linked to his carnal condition. This characteristic of flesh ensures the originality of the Eucharistic presence. Although of a contrary condition vis-à-vis spirit, this presence is open to the Spirit, and filled with the same.

The two presences are not in competition. They are not reciprocally damaging. The Eucharistic presence is that of Christ, with the proper characteristic of being the presence of the incarnate Son. This presence ever maintains its unique character; but it is enriched by the presence of the Holy Spirit, which is necessary if flesh is to enjoy a full spiritual efficacy.

Chapter 5

Jesus Really Present according to the Doctrine of the Church

The real presence of the body and blood of Christ in the Eucharist, clearly enunciated by Jesus' words according to the testimonials of the Gospels and Saint Paul, has been received in the tradition of the Church as a truth of faith. It has been abundantly asserted and commented on in the teachings of the Fathers. Since the patristic period, the doctrine has developed as a result of certain controversies, with the definitive voice being that of the Council of Trent.

The Council of Trent

Real Presence

The Council of Trent defines the real presence as a truth of faith. In its doctrinal chapter, it stresses that, in this area, there has not as yet been a clear, precise conciliar teaching: "In the first place, the Sacred Council openly and simply asserts that in the precious sacrament of the Most Holy Eucharist, after the consecration of the bread and wine, our Lord Jesus Christ, true God and true human being, is contained truly, really, and substantially, under the appearance [*specie*] of those sensible things" (DS 1636).

The three adverbs "truly, really, and substantially" are not intended as having different meanings. They are used simply to assert the reality of Christ's presence. We find them again in the canon: "In the most holy sacrament of the Eucharist are contained, truly, really, and substantially, the body and blood, in union with the soul and the divinity, of our Lord Jesus Christ, and hence the whole Christ" (Canon 1, DS 1651).

The council responds to the objection deriving from the presence of Christ in heaven: "There is no contradiction whatever in the fact that our Savior forever sits at the right hand of the Father in heaven, according to an existence natural to him, and that nevertheless, for us, he is found in many other places, as well, sacramentally present in his substance, with an existence that our words cannot adequately express, but that our intellects, enlightened by faith, can nevertheless acknowledge and that we must firmly believe as a thing possible to God" (DS 1636). In asserting that no incompatibility exists, the council suggests the reason: seated at the right hand of the Father, the Savior has the power to become present in the sacrament.

As for the form of presence, the council underscores its mysterious character. It is a form of existence that our words have difficulty expressing, but that our intelligence, enlightened by faith, can know. This means that Christ's presence in the sacrament will always remain a mystery. We assert it by virtue of the light of faith, and we make an effort to specify its meaning. But we are dealing with a truth that surpasses us. It is enough to assert that it does not contain any contradiction. It is above reason, but does not contradict it.

The council teaches this truth not in virtue of anything that is obvious to reason, but because "it transmits, concerning this true and divine sacrament of the Eucharist, the holy and authentic doctrine that the Catholic Church, instructed by our Lord Jesus Christ himself, by way of his apostles and the Holy Spirit, who intimates all truth to it in the course of time (see John 14:26), has ever preserved it, and will preserve it to the end of the world" (DS 1635).

It is the tradition of the Church, then, that decisively imposes the affirmation of the real presence.

Integral Presence of Christ

The council asserts not only the real presence of Christ's body and blood. It declares that Jesus Christ, "true God and true man," is present. The entire person of Christ, integrally, is present. According to the faith of the Church, "from the moment of the consecration, the true body of Our Lord and his true blood are present, in union with his soul and divinity." The soul and divinity are present, therefore, and cannot be separated from the body and blood.

Speaking of the reason for the presence, however, the council makes certain distinctions.

> The body is under the species of bread, and the blood under that of wine, by virtue of the words, but the body is under the species of wine, and the blood under that of bread, and the soul under both species, in virtue of that natural connection and concomitance by which the parts of Christ our Lord, who, "being raised from the dead, will never die again" (Rom. 6:9), are linked with one another; as for the divinity, it is present there on account of its wondrous hypostatic union with the body and the soul. (DS 1640)

The council comes to the conclusion of the total presence of Christ under each species: "Therefore it is absolutely true that he is contained under the one species as under the other and under both. Indeed the total and integral Christ exists under the species of bread and under any particle of the said species, as the whole Christ exists under the species of wine and under all of its parts" (DS 1641). Canon 3 resumes the assertion: "In the venerable sacrament of the Eucharist, the whole Christ is contained under each species, and if these are divided, under each part of each species" (DS 1653).

Furthermore, the indivisible oneness of Christ means that where the body of Christ is found, there also will his blood be present, along with his soul and his divinity. But a distinction must be made between the presence resulting from the words of consecration and that due the constitutive oneness of the person of Christ. The body and blood are rendered present owing to the words pronounced over the bread and wine. Still, it is important to observe that the body is present under the species of wine on the basis of the connection obtaining between the body and the blood, and not strictly in virtue of the words of consecration as such. The same is the case with the blood, present under the species of bread in virtue of the permanent bond prevailing between the blood and the body.

Even more important is the presence of Christ's soul, by virtue of its indissoluble union with the body, a oneness definitively acquired at the moment of the Resurrection. There was a separation at the moment of Jesus' death, but we must recall that the body given as Eucharistic food is the body in its glorious state, a state that reunited his body and soul at the moment of the Resurrection and that makes any separation in the future impossible.

Finally, above all else, there is the presence of the divinity. Body and soul in Christ belong to the divine person of the Son. Their presence has meaning only as the actual presence of Christ's person. The divinity designates the divine nature, inasmuch as, through the hypostatic union, divine nature and human nature are united in the hypostasis or person of Christ.

The Truth Defined

The Council of Trent teaches the "transubstantiation" as a truth indissolubly united to that of the real presence. What is being taught by the council here is a truth of faith and not a mere philosophical opinion. Indeed, the Church has always believed that, through the consecration of the bread and wine, a transformation of the entire substance of the bread and wine into the body and blood of Christ is realized.

It is important to specify precisely the truth defined by the council. It is a matter of a conversion from one substance into another, with the "species" of bread and wine remaining intact.

1. The term "conversion" used by the council means simply "change." It does not imply any indication of the nature of the change, nor of the manner in which it is effected. The council does not offer any particular explanation and limits itself to asserting "what essentially constitutes a change, that is, the succession of two things, one of which takes the place of the other."[11]

2. The change is from one substance to another. The term "substance" had been used in various philosophical systems before the council, especially in the distinction between substance and accidents proposed by Aristotle and adopted by Saint Thomas. As is shown by the intentions expressed during the conciliar debates, it is certain that the council did not seek to link the expression of the dogma of the transubstantiation to any particular philoso-

---

11. L. Godefroy, *Dictionnaire de théologie catholique*, 5:1349.

phy. "The council adheres to no theory and imposes no system" (ibid., 1348).

In the term "substance" we should see only what common sense sees there, that is, that altogether elusive foundation that science does not reach, that observation does not discover, that the senses do not perceive, and that reason nonetheless tells us exists in all things as point of attachment and ultimate rationale of phenomena and properties: that is, in a word, reality as distinguished from appearances (ibid., 1349).

Thus we are to understand substance as the fundamental reality underlying appearances. In the sacrament of the Eucharist, a change occurs such that the reality of the bread gives place to the reality of the body of Christ.

3. The change leaves the "species" of bread and wine unaltered, but only the species. Nothing subsists of the substance of the bread and wine, since by virtue of the words of consecration only the substance of the body and blood of Christ is present.

Let us observe that the council speaks not of "accidents," but of "species." The term "accident" could have designated, according to Aristotelian philosophy, what remains of the bread and wine after the consecration. The council deliberately avoids using this term, lest it give the appearance of embracing Aristotelian philosophy. It speaks of "species," a term not borrowed from any philosophical system, and one that indicates sensible appearances, but appearances that are real as appearances, which continue to be the object of observation of the senses and are not only phantasms or illusions. "The appearances are everything we see, everything we observe or experience, everything that falls in any manner under the senses. All of this subsists, because for our experience, everything remains as if the consecration had changed nothing" (ibid.).

Theologians have sought a better clarification of everything signified by the change of substance together with the persistence of the species. But the situation at hand has no parallel in the order of nature. The conversion from one substance to another is "wondrous and unique," says the council, and therefore can be accepted and understood only in an exceptional sense. The mystery abides, although it does not forbid us from exerting all our efforts in order the better to gather its import.

The Term "Transubstantiation"

The term "transubstantiation" is an absolutely appropriate expression. The Church uses this term to express the change of the consecration in all precision. It is not regarded as a concept belonging to a philosophical system: the term "substance" contained in it represents no specific link with a particular theory.

Later, the Synod of Pistoia tried to eliminate the term from the presentation of the Eucharistic doctrine. While affirming the real presence of Christ under the species after the consecration of the Mass and admitting the disappearance of the substance of bread and wine, that synod avoided speaking of transubstantiation and of substantial conversion of the bread into the body and the wine into the blood. The intentional omission was expressly condemned by Pope Pius VI in 1794, because it seemed to open up to discussion once again not only the term, but the very doctrine of transubstantiation (DS 2629).

In doctrinal development, the word "transubstantiation" was accepted as best adapted to express the faith of the Church relative to what occurs at the moment of the consecration of the bread and wine. From its appearance, in the twelfth century, it had seen a rapid propagation, since it is most appropriate for making the essential core of the doctrine understood.

It preserves its value, indicating the depth of the change of the fundamental reality — or substance — of the bread into the fundamental reality of the body of Christ. Some have held this term too complicated or too difficult to explain. But the change of one reality into another can be understood with sufficient facility. Withal, the assertion remains inevitably wrapped in the mystery of the Eucharist.

Even today we see no term better adapted to explain the Church's doctrine.

Foundation and Development

In Scripture

Ultimately, the doctrine of the transubstantiation has its foundation in the words of Jesus, "This [is] my body," and "This [is] my blood." Actually these words simply assert the presence of the body and the presence of the blood, and this supposes that the bread has yielded its place to the body and the wine to the blood.

More exactly: Jesus does not say, "This bread is my body," or "This wine is my blood." In saying "This," he gives no previous determination to what he is holding. And his words assign, as the sole determination, the body and blood.

We must conclude that what were first bread and wine in virtue of his words have become body and blood, but preserving the sensible appearance of bread and wine. In the words of consecration, the transubstantiation is explicitly pronounced: the change of the reality of the bread and wine into the reality of the body and blood.

In Tradition

The Fathers of the Church assert the change of the bread into the body of Christ: the bread and wine are changed or transformed into the body and blood of Christ. The bread and wine cease to be bread and wine, and instead of them we have the body and blood. "What seems bread, is not bread, even if it seems such to the taste, but the body of Christ, and what seems wine is not wine, even though it has its taste, but the blood of Christ."[12] "Before the sacramental words, this bread is bread. Once the consecration occurs, the bread becomes the body of Christ."[13] In order to describe this change, the Fathers invoke the analogy of the transformation of water into wine at the wedding in Cana.

The expression "substantial conversion" appears at the Council of Rome (1079), which put an end to the controversy with Berengarius.

The term "transubstantiation" is found for the first time in Rolando Bandinelli (the future Pope Alexander III). The spread of the term was rapid. The Fourth Council of the Lateran (1215) used the verb "transubstantiate."

---

12. Cyril of Jerusalem, Cat. 4, 9; *PG* 33:1104.
13. Ambrose, *PL* 16:439–40.

Chapter 6

The Eucharistic Sacrifice

True Sacrifice

"In the Mass, a true and authentic sacrifice is offered to God," and "this offering does not consist only in the fact that Christ is given to us as food."[14] "The sacrifice of the Mass is not only a sacrifice of praise and thanksgiving, nor a simple commemoration of the sacrifice accomplished on the Cross, but a propitiatory sacrifice."[15] It is with these words that the Council of Trent attests to the sacrificial value of the Eucharistic celebration.

True and Unique Sacrifice

Since, under the Old Testament, as the Apostle Paul testifies, on account of the impotence of the Levitical sacrifice, there was no perfect sacrifice, it was necessary in the disposition of God, the Father of mercies (2 Cor. 1:3), that another priest come forward, "according to the order of Melchizedek" (Gen. 14:18, Ps. 109:4, Heb. 7:11), our Lord Jesus Christ, in a condition to "perfect for all time those who are sanctified" (see Heb. 10:14). Therefore our God and Lord had to "offer himself once for all" (see Heb. 7:27), dying on the altar of the Cross to realize for them an everlasting redemption.

This appeal to the value of the Cross could readily be accepted by the Reformers, who do not deny such a value. Later, however, we have what more directly regards the Eucharist: "Still, since his death would not put an end to his priesthood (see Heb. 7:24), at the Last Supper, on the night he was betrayed, he wished to leave the Church, his beloved spouse, a visible sacrifice, such as human nature required. In it would have to be represented the sacrifice of

---

14. Council of Trent, Canon 1, DS 1751.
15. Canon 3, DS 1753.

blood that was about to be accomplished one time forever on the Cross, whose recall would be perpetuated to the end of the ages (see 1 Cor. 11:23–24) and whose salutary virtue would have to be applied to redemption from the sins we commit every day." The Eucharistic sacrifice was that given by Christ to the Church, then. It is by the Church, then, and not only by Christ himself, that the sacrifice is reproduced to the end of the ages.

The council specifies the meaning of this sacrifice by underscoring the behavior of Christ:

> Declaring that he had been appointed "a priest forever according to the order of Melchizedek" (Ps. 110:4), he offered to God the Father his body and blood under the species of bread and wine, and under the same species he gave them as food to the Apostles, constituting them at that moment priests of the New Testament. To them and to their successors in the priesthood he gave the order to offer them, with the words "Do this in remembrance of me" (Luke 22:19), as the Church has always understood and taught.
>
> (DS 1739–40)

Scriptural Foundations

Gospel Witness. Jesus made no doctrinal declaration on the sacrifice offered in the Eucharist, but the words of institution sufficiently demonstrate that it is a matter of a true, propitiatory sacrifice.

The words "This [is] my body, [which is] given for you" (Luke 22:19) attest that the body is not only given as food to those present, but that it is given "for" them, that is, in sacrifice.

The words pronounced for the consecration of the wine allude to sacrifice even more explicitly: "This [is] my blood of the covenant, [which is] poured out for many" (Mark 14:24, Matt. 26:28). The mere fact of the use of terms employed in Exodus 24:8 for the striking of the covenant with Moses is significant for its allusion to sacrifice. Here we have the true sacrifice that realizes the ancient prefiguration and ratifies the sole real covenant for the benefit of the multitude, that is, all humanity.

"Give" is the verb used by Jesus to designate his sacrifice. "The

Son of Man came not to be served but to serve, and to give his life as a ransom for many" (Mark 10:45, Matt. 20:28). The promise reported by John confirms the intention of sacrifice: "The bread that I will give for the life of the world is my flesh" (John 6:51). The term "flesh" is particularly indicated when the intent is to designate sacrifice. This sacrifice has a value that far surpasses participation in the meal: "For the life of the world" is the equivalent of "for many."

The formula of the consecration of the wine in Matthew (26:28) includes an addition expressing more directly the expiatory or propitiatory nature of the sacrifice: blood "poured out... for the forgiveness of sins." This addition only emphasizes what was already implicit with reference to the blood of the covenant, spilled for the multitude.

Witness of Saint Paul. Reporting the words of consecration of the bread, Paul implies its sacrificial intent with the expression "my body that is for you" (1 Cor. 11:24).

He produces the proclamation of the death of Christ that is presented at every Eucharistic meal: "As often as you eat this bread and drink the cup, you proclaim the Lord's death until he comes" (1 Cor. 11:26). This proclamation complements Jesus' words, "Do this [...] in remembrance of me" (1 Cor. 11:24, 25). What we have, then, is a proclamation intended to repeat what Christ did at the Last Supper, that is, make an offering of the redemptive sacrifice, but an offering that is no longer bloody, having a character now purely ritual or sacramental.

Witness of the Letter to the Hebrews. The Letter to the Hebrews, the only New Testament writing to set forth Christ's sacrifice in a systematic manner, includes an observation that helps show the superiority of the Christian priesthood: "We have an altar from which those who officiate in the tent have no right to eat" (Heb. 13:10). It would seem that the author sought to stress the fact that Jewish priests were not permitted to approach the Eucharist. "Eat" seems to refer to the Eucharistic meal, which is taken at an altar. An altar is linked to sacrifice: The Eucharist feeds on Christ's sacrifice and hence has a sacrificial character. However, the sacrifice could be simply that of the Cross. The allusion is too vague to be available to a precise interpretation.

Foundations of Tradition

In the first postbiblical Christian writings, the Eucharist was seen not only as a meal but as a sacrifice.

The *Didachē*, for example, states literally that the Eucharistic celebration is a sacrifice. Saint Justin frequently makes the same statement.

Subsequent tradition, with Saint Irenaeus, Origen, and Saint Cyprian, preserves this doctrine. Origen more particularly asserts the propitiatory nature of the Eucharistic sacrifice.

We could cite many testimonials throughout the centuries. We shall limit ourselves here to citing Paul VI's encyclical *Mysterium Fidei:* "Most of all, it helps to recall what is as the synthesis and summit of this doctrine, that which in the Eucharistic mystery is represented in a wondrous way: the sacrifice of the Cross, once for all consummated on Calvary. It is constantly recalled to our memory, and its salutary virtue is applied in the remission of the sins that are daily committed."[16]

Sacramental Sacrifice

The assertion of the Eucharistic sacrifice inevitably poses a problem. How is one to define this sacrifice vis-à-vis the sacrifice of the Cross? How can it be seen as identical with the sacrifice of Calvary, given that its purpose is to represent and produce it, and how is it distinguished from that sacrifice?

Identity and Difference

A response in principle is furnished us by the Council of Trent, when it treats of the Eucharist as a propitiatory sacrifice: "There is one single and unique victim: he is the same who now makes his offering by way of the ministry of priests, the one who offered himself once on the Cross. Only the manner of offering differs" (DS 1743).

As to the victim or object of the sacrifice, identity prevails. The offering presented in the Eucharist is the offering of Christ. In the Eucharistic sacrifice, Christ himself is offered. It is always he, and

---

16. *AAS* 57 (1965), no. 11.

he alone, who is the price paid for our salvation. Therefore in the Eucharistic celebration the body and blood of Christ are rendered present: it is they, with the person of the Savior to whom they belong, who are presented as an offering to the Father for the salvation of humanity and for all of the graces bound to this salvation. In the Eucharist they are given as food and drink.

Likewise with regard to him who makes the offering, identity prevails. It is Christ who offers himself. At the Last Supper, he himself made this offering by pronouncing the words of consecration over the bread and wine. In subsequent Eucharistic celebrations, no longer being on earth, Christ would not be able to perform the visible act of offering. But he works by way of the ministry of priests: owing to this visible mediation, he repeats in an invisible way the act of offering. And this corresponds to his order to repeat what he does: "Do this in commemoration of me."

Some theologians have discussed whether one must think that the Council of Trent intended to speak of an actual offering made by Christ at every Mass, or whether it limited itself to defining a simple virtual oblation, that is, an oblation or offering made by the Church in virtue of the power conferred upon it by Christ. The terms used by the council seem to impose rather the definition of an act of offering performed by Christ, even though the act is actually performed thanks to the ministry of priests: it is not a matter simply of an act performed by the Church thanks to the power given to it by Christ. In saying that the one who offered himself once on the Cross is the same one that now makes this offering through the ministry of priests, the council was insisting on the identity of the subject of the offering and hence defining an act of offering performed by Christ at every Mass. The involvement of Christ in the Eucharistic sacrifice is not inferior to his involvement in the sacrifice of the Cross, because the same one makes the offering just as the same one is the victim.

The sole difference between the two sacrifices consists in the "manner of offering." The sacrifice of the Cross was a bloody immolation, while the Eucharistic sacrifice is of a ritual order and excludes any shedding of blood. Besides, the Eucharistic sacrifice has the distinctive element of an offering of the body and blood of Christ under the species of bread and wine, which are sacramental signs. Thus, we can define the Eucharistic sacrifice as a sacramental sacrifice; and in this it differs from the sacrifice of the Cross. The Church's worship multiplies the sacramental sacrifice, while that of the Cross is unique. On Calvary, the sacrifice which obtains the salvation of the world was accomplished once and for all. That sacrifice is a historical event, which, inserted as it is in an altogether precise moment of history and in altogether determinate circumstances, is no longer repeated as such. It will forever preserve a unique character.

The sacramental sacrifice, by contrast, celebrated in reference to this unique and exceptional sacrifice in history, is destined to be repeated to foster the growth of the Church. It is therefore quite different from the sacrifice of the Cross: and yet it is in strict relationship with it, and depends entirely on it, since the victim is the same and he who offers it is the same. The sacramental sacrifice ritually reproduces the redemptive sacrifice in the world.

Representation of the Redemptive Sacrifice

In order to express the relationship between the Eucharistic sacrifice and that of the Cross, the term "representation" is used, "re-presentation." The council asserts that Christ wished to leave the Church "a visible sacrifice, . . . in which would be represented the bloody sacrifice that was to be accomplished once for all on the Cross, and whose memory would be perpetuated to the end of the ages" (DS 1740). The encyclical *Mysterium Fidei*, as well, speaks of what "in the Eucharistic mystery is represented in a wondrous way: the sacrifice of the Cross."[17] Vatican II and Trent both assert that, in the Eucharist, "the victory and triumph of his death are again made present."[18]

The verb "represent," however, should be understood in its stronger acceptation: "represent," here, signifies "render present once again" the sacrifice of the Cross. It is not a matter of a "representation" that would be limited to remembering or celebrating the memory of an event in the past. The representation consists

17. *AAS* 57 (1960), no. 11.
18. Vatican Council II, *Sacrosanctum Concilium* (Constitution on the Sacred Liturgy), no. 6; quoting the Council of Trent, *Decree on the Eucharist*, chap. 5.

in a sacramental reproduction of the sacrifice of the Cross: it renders that sacrifice present in such a way as to apply its fruits to the Church.

With his act of offering, Jesus renews his sacrifice in an unbloody manner, without executioners or natural death, since the essence of the redemptive sacrifice is of an interior, spiritual nature: a will of oblation in the immolation of the Cross.

This act is accomplished by Christ in his heavenly condition as glorious Savior, whose sacrifice has already been consummated: it cannot acquire new value, but can only be applied more broadly. The new offering in the Eucharist therefore draws all of its value from the sacrifice of the Cross and applies its merits.

Christ renews the offering of the sacrifice sacramentally through the ministry of the priest. The whole raison d'être of this representation of the salvific act is in its sacramental nature. In itself, the sacrifice of the Cross was perfect and sufficed for obtaining all graces for salvation and the spiritual life of humanity. In its sacramental representation, it pours forth its fruits more widely.

The Sacrifice Signified and Realized by the Consecration

The essence of the sacrifice is found in the consecration of the Mass. Indeed, the words pronounced over the bread and wine constitute the memorial that Christ has entrusted to his disciples. The Eucharistic offering of the sacrifice, then, is accomplished through the consecration. We cannot identify it with a rite: considered in itself, the offering of the bread and wine do not realize the sacrifice, but prepare it and initiate it.

Thus we must see the words "This is my body" and "This is my blood" as the efficacious or effective sign of the sacrifice. It is an efficacious sign in that it realizes what it signifies.

This notion of efficacious sign is linked to the notion of sacrament, which is defined as an efficacious sign of grace. In the case of the efficacious sign of the words of consecration, the sign is not properly one of grace, but of the personal offering of the one who is the source of grace. We may conclude that the concept of sacrament is verified in the most eminent manner. The sacramental sacrifice is the sacrament par excellence, the sign of Christ's offering and presence.

The words of consecration have often been interpreted as a sign of sacrifice because of the separation of the species: the separation of the bread from the wine, with the double consecration, appears as a sign of the separation of the body from the blood and hence as sign of death, a sign of sacrifice.

But, while ascribing a value to this symbolism, we must take care to observe that the sign of sacrifice already emerges from the words "This is my body, [which is] given for you" (Luke 22:19). Even independently of the consecration of the wine, these words denote the body given in sacrifice. We may add that the word used by Jesus, "my flesh," would strongly suggest the flesh of sacrificial victims.

For their part, even considered in isolation, the words of the consecration of the wine, "This is my blood of the covenant, which is poured out for many" (Mark 14:24, Matt. 26:28), express a patent reference to sacrifice.

Thus, it is not the simple separation of the species that constitute the sign of sacrifice, but the rite of the consecration in all of its parts and aspects, with the words that assert the presence of the body and blood. These words are an affirmation of presence, but such presence comes as a gift that Christ makes of his person, and more specifically of his flesh and blood. They are therefore the expression of an offering: with his words, pronounced by the priest in the name of Christ, the offering is realized that renews the sacrifice of the Cross or that reproduces it for the interest and welfare of the Church.

Some theories that defined the sacrifice through a change in the thing offered proposed, as a sign of the Eucharistic sacrifice, the transubstantiation. But the essence of the sacrifice does not consist in the change, and besides, in the transubstantiation it is the bread or wine that is changed. But neither the bread nor the wine is the victim. In the Eucharistic sacrifice, the victim is the same as in the sacrifice of the Cross. In each case, declares the council, the victim is one and unique.

Naturally, the transubstantiation enters into the sign of sacrifice, but not by reason of a change in the victim. The victim is implicit in the offering made by Christ of himself by giving his body and blood. And it is this offering, signified by the words of the consecration, that realizes the sacrifice.

Offering of the Glorious Christ

The sacramental sacrifice renders present the offering of Christ, more especially the offering of the glorious Christ and not only Christ caught up in the drama of the Cross. Subsequently to that drama, the sacrifice has indeed received a complement that has manifested its efficacy. Receiving his Son in the world to come, the Father has covered him with the divine glory. Previously, indeed, Jesus had announced on several occasions the resurrection of the Son of Man on the third day. He had wished to convey that the death he was foretelling was inseparable from its glorious requital. The sacrifice must be confronted only in the prospect of that happy outcome.

Accordingly, the Christian message may never separate from one another the death and resurrection of Jesus. The two events are indissolubly united, and only the Resurrection can shed light on the sense of Jesus' death. In the Eucharist, the sacrifice could not have repeated the offering of Jesus' death without its indispensable counterpart, his glorification.

We can recall, furthermore, that Jesus himself, in foretelling the Eucharist, had called attention to the glorious state of the Son of Man as a presupposition of the nutritive value of his body and blood: the state that he was to acquire in the Ascension must be the previous condition of the life-giving power that would be expressed in the Eucharistic meal. Therefore we must see a certain anticipation of the Savior's glorious state at the moment of the celebration of the Last Supper.

Only the glorious Christ possesses the power to renew the offering of his body and blood in sacrifice. This is the reason why the celebration of the Eucharist is not held only in memory of the Passion of Christ, but also in memory of his resurrection and his ascension.

The Christ who comes upon the altar is the risen Savior. And it is as risen Savior that he offers himself as food and drink in the Eucharistic meal. But it is true that he is the same Christ who was born of a Virgin, that he lived a life on earth similar to ours, and that he devoted himself to the discharge of his mission all the way to his raising up on the Cross. But our communion with him is in the more exalted life of his heavenly state, a life that flows to us from the gifts of the Holy Spirit.

It is important, then, to complete what we have said about the sign of the sacrifice in the Eucharist. The double consecration of the bread and wine is not only a consecration of the Eucharistic species in separation, but is also a sign of union, because it is a sign of the union of body and blood, a union that recalls Christ's victory over death with his resurrection.

The words pronounced by Jesus, "This [is] my body," signify a living flesh, as is confirmed by the destination of that flesh itself as food that maintains life and gives it growth. The words "This is the cup of my blood" make us think, through the sign of wine, of a certain spiritual inebriation. In the words of the consecration, then, we can find the sign of a sacrifice consummated through our own entry into the state of a more exalted life, a sharing in the glorious state of Christ.

It will be in order to underscore the importance of this glorious state of Christ in the offering of the Eucharist. This offering, considered simply in terms of the redemptive drama and with reference to the cruel sufferings undergone by the Savior, would have called for a climate of struggle: the memorial would have had to be essentially sorrowful. Instead, the contrary occurs. Because the offering is made by the glorious Christ, it implies the transformation of suffering into joy.

The Eucharist is celebrated as a festival, in a climate of joy. Our gladness confirms the fundamental truth of the divine triumph over all of the forces that place humanity's destiny in danger.

Drawing its energy from Christ's resurrection, the Eucharist gains for humanity a renewal of its noblest life. It shows that the effect of the sacrament of redemption is not limited to the remission of sins, but consists mainly in the development of Christ's divine life, a life aroused and maintained by the Holy Spirit. The strength of the Resurrection heals all of the frailties and weaknesses of human life. The power of the Ascension, which also belongs to the glorious Christ, is capable of restoring all that has been torn down or paralyzed and of elevating human beings to the highest level.

This is the manner in which the relationship of the Eucharist with the work of salvation acquires all of its meaning. The Eucharist not only reproduces sacramentally the sublime, heroic offering on Calvary that changed the face of the world, obtaining the divine forgiveness in abundance. It is also nourished by the mystery of the Resurrection, which even today continues the work of creation of a new humanity. Humanity receives from the mystery of the Ascension the strength of a Christ seated at the right hand of the Father and sharing all of the power of the Father. Since Christ renews his offering, the Resurrection applies its proper source and the Ascension its thrust to the heavens by lifting up the whole weight of humanity and renewing the forces of human existence. To say that Jesus is the very one who offers the Eucharist is to believe in the value of his offering, which, in a climate of gladness and enthusiasm, leads all human beings to the building of a better world.

Sacrifice of Christ, Sacrifice of the Church

Involvement of the Church in the Sacrifice

The Eucharistic sacrifice is the sacrifice of Christ: Christ is the victim and also the priest, the principal, sovereign priest, who works through ministers who act in his name.

But the Eucharistic sacrifice is at the same time a sacrifice of the Church. And this is its whole raison d'être: the sacramental sacrifice exists only for the good of the Church and its members. To what purpose, indeed, would the offering of the sacrifice of the Cross be renewed if not in order that it become the sacrifice of the Church? The sacrifice accomplished on Calvary has no need of being repeated. It is unique and was offered once for all, acquiring for humanity the graces necessary for salvation. To reproduce that sacrifice over the course of time would have no meaning, unless this reproduction or "re-presentation" meant an involvement of the Church in that sacrifice. This supposes that the Church is in a position to make Christ's sacrifice its own and to enter into the association that that sacrifice involves.

Thus, the Eucharistic sacrifice is not a simple repetition of Christ's offering on Calvary, but an appropriation, on the part of the Church, of that offering, with a view to a wider fecundity. This appropriation of Christ's sacrifice on the part of the Church is an objective appropriation, in the sense that, sacramentally, the Savior's offering becomes that of the Church, through the execution of the rite instituted by Jesus at the Last Supper. The words of consecration realize the sacrifice of Christ as the sacrifice of the Church.

This objective appropriation, guaranteed by the rite, has a tendency to be completed in a subjective appreciation: that is, the priest and the faithful who participate in the Eucharist are invited to associate themselves, with their personal dispositions, to the offering of the redemptive sacrifice. The Eucharistic celebration tends to lead them to share the Savior's sentiments and will of oblation.

Cooperation of the Church in the Eucharistic Sacrifice

The doctrine enunciated by Vatican II on the liturgy relates to the Eucharist:

> Christ indeed always associates the Church with himself in the truly great work of giving perfect praise to God and making men holy. The Church is his dearly beloved bride who calls to her Lord, and through him offers worship to the eternal Father. (*Sacrosanctum Concilium*, no. 7)

Thus, "every liturgical celebration . . . is an action of Christ the Priest and of his body the Church" (ibid.; DS 4008).

Cooperation through the Ministry of the Priest

The cooperation of the Church in the sacrifice is expressed above all through the ministry of the priest. It is the priest who offers the sacrifice ministerially. He is only a minister, in the sense that he is at the service of Christ: he pronounces the words of consecration only in the name of Christ. In saying, "This is my body," and "This is the cup of my blood," he renders present the body and blood of Christ. He can pronounce these words only by virtue of the power he has received in priestly ordination. This power has been conferred upon him by the authority of the Church: in exercising it in the name of the Church, he also exercises it in the name of Christ.

The accomplishment of the Eucharistic sacrifice, then, requires a specific commitment on the part of the ministerial priesthood. Some have made bold to attribute the power to celebrate the Eucharist to all Christians, in the name of the universal priesthood. The encyclical *Mediator Dei*, in 1941, reacted against this excess, recalling the traditional position of the Church on this point:

> The fact that the faithful take part in the Eucharistic sacrifice, however, does not mean that they enjoy priestly powers. . . . There are those who, embracing errors already condemned, teach that the New Testament knows only a priesthood that regards all of the baptized, and that the precept given by Jesus to the Apostles at the Last Supper, to do what he had done, refers directly to the whole Church of Christians. . . . Therefore they maintain that only the people enjoy a true priestly power, while the priest only exercises an office committed to him by the community.[19]

Here the encyclical recalls the principle "that the priest represents the people because he represents the person of our Lord Jesus Christ as head of all of the members and offers himself for these members" (ibid., no. 69).

There is a power of offering the Eucharistic sacrifice in the name of Christ, then, which is exclusively that of the priest.

Recently, as well, this necessity for the intervention of the priest in the celebration of the Eucharist has created certain problems. In many areas, the decline in the rate of vocations has deprived some parish communities of the priestly ministry. Sunday assemblies in the absence of a priest have become more frequent. These assemblies pray together, read Scripture, and distribute Communion. But they are not able to participate in the celebration of the Eucharistic mystery, that is, in the most important act of Christian worship. The consecration of the bread and wine and their transformation into the body and blood of Christ are not possible when a priest is not present. We can understand that Christians of deep faith in the Eucharist suffer particularly when they are deprived of it. However, this situation can also awaken Christians'

---

19. *AAS* 39 (1941), no. 68.

sense of responsibility in the sowing and maturation of the seed that is a vocation. In the divine design, these communities should develop a deep Christian life in families and individuals, in order that youth may hear the resounding call to the priestly life and that call may find fertile soil for a generous and persevering response. The spiritual drama of the communities deprived of the Eucharist on account of the scarcity of clergy can occasion an appreciation of the importance of the presence and mission of priests, which are indispensable for a development of all of the spiritual riches borne by Christ to the world and, in particular, for the multiplication of Eucharistic celebrations.

Participation of All the Faithful

Now that we have acknowledged the value of the priestly ministry, it will be equally important to stress the value of the participation of all the faithful at the Eucharistic celebration, given that the entire Church is involved in it.

This participation has for its foundation the universal priesthood granted to all of the baptized, a priesthood that consists in a consecration, bestowed at the baptismal font, that renders them capable of the whole development of the sacramental life and, more in particular, a true involvement in the offering of the Eucharistic sacrifice. "The faithful join in the offering of the Eucharist by virtue of their royal priesthood," says Vatican II (*Lumen Gentium*, no. 10). Pius XII had already explained that the faithful offer the sacrifice, not only through the hands of the priest, but also, in a certain fashion, in union with him.

> Thus, when it is said that the people make the offering together with the priest, it is not asserted that the members of the Church, and not only the priest himself, perform the visible liturgical rite, which belongs alone to the minister of God deputed for this, but that they unite their vows of praise, impetration, expiation, and thanksgiving to the intention of the priest, indeed, of the High Priest himself, that they may be presented to God the Father in the same oblation of the victim, and this in the external rite of the priest. In fact, it is necessary that the external rite of the sacrifice manifest inter-

nal worship by its nature; and the sacrifice of the new law
denotes that supreme service with which the principal offerer
himself, Christ, and with him and through him all of his mystical members, honor God in due fashion.

(Mediator Dei, no. 76)

The encyclical emphasizes that the sacrifice cannot attain its purpose except through participation in the immolation. "In order for
the oblation, then, with which the faithful offer in this sacrifice
the divine victim to the heavenly Father, to have its full effect, another thing is necessary: that they immolate themselves as victims"
(ibid., no. 81).

When those solemn words are pronounced, "Through him,
with him, in him, in the unity of the Holy Spirit, all glory and
honor is yours, almighty Father, for ever and ever," to which
words the people respond, "Amen," let Christians not forget to offer themselves and their concerns, sorrows, anxieties,
miseries, and needs with the divine head crucified.

(Ibid., no. 86)

The notion of sacramental sacrifice is understood in its require-
ments and on the basis of its finality or purpose. The sacramental
rite is essential, since through the consecration of the bread and
wine the offering of the redemptive sacrifice is reproduced. But this
rite has for its object to lend Christians a share in the one sacrifice
of the Cross, in such a way as to be fully a sacrifice of the Church
besides the sacrifice of Christ.

The ritual offering, then, requires a living participation on the
part of the faithful as their personal offering. Christians should not
attend the Mass as an act of worship that is without their interior
participation. If the rite remains external, it does not attain its object, which is to awaken an interior disposition corresponding to
the exterior action. The Eucharistic sacrifice is celebrated in order
to involve Christians in the fundamental movement of the offering
of Christ.

The problem posed by each Eucharistic celebration to those who
attend it, then, is that of the offering to be associated to the offering of the Savior. All are invited to ask themselves what they ought

to offer. Without this personal involvement in the offering, the sacrifice fails to attain its objective, because the offering of Christ is sacramentally renewed only because we can unite ourselves to him.

True, the whole Christian life, even without the Eucharist, consists in union with the person of Christ and his salvific work. Still, the Eucharist tends to give a more concrete form to such a union, placing before our eyes the offering that has gained the salvation of the world. The Eucharist includes, more precisely, the invitation to offer all that in our lives that is sorrowful or painful, with our gaze fixed on the heroic offering of Calvary. Painful as our sufferings may be, we should "intend" not only our sufferings properly so called, but also our anguish, our sometimes vexing concerns, our moral situations with all of the interior dramas that explode outwardly or that remain concealed, our tensions of every kind in our relationships with others. All that is experienced in our daily round deserves to be carried as an offering to the Eucharist, in order to receive there a higher dignity through an assimilation to the redemptive suffering of Christ.

The problem of personal offering in the Eucharistic celebration can have a response of great generosity when the supreme offering of Jesus arouses or fosters commitment to a life in which the total gift of self is expressed, or else to an activity that requires an exceptional dedication. But the problem also arises for the most common circumstances of life. Difficulties are not lacking. They may provoke complaints and regrets, but the Eucharistic sacrifice tends to foster a spirit of offering that accepts the obstacles more willingly and is able to see in them the possibility of a deeper love.

The sacramental nature of the sacrifice could give the impression of an orientation opposed to mysticism, since the rite has an objective value independent of the subjective dispositions of the individual. On the contrary, we must observe that, in its objective reality, the sacrament calls for an intense subjective participation in the mystery of the redemptive offering. This participation takes on a mystical aspect, thanks to a more intimate union with the person of Jesus. It tends to foster the most extreme manifestations of this union, through a sharing in the offering and the desire to contribute to the spread of salvific grace in the world.

Therefore, even though it is enclosed in a particular sphere of spirituality, the Eucharistic sacrifice is destined to transform Christians' most ordinary life by communicating to them the breath of Christ's redemptive offering.

Fruit of the Eucharistic Sacrifice

The sacrificial offering of Christ, realized in the consecration through the ministry of the priest, yields a particular fruit, which is gained through the simple implementation of the sacramental act. This is the fruit that theologians call *ex opere operato*.

All of the fruit of the Eucharistic celebration comes from the sacrifice of the Cross: indeed, the Eucharistic sacrifice only renders present the one redemptive sacrifice, the source of all graces. The sole value of the Mass is that which derives from the oblation of Calvary.

Theological reflection has seen a fourfold efficacy in the Mass in virtue of the fourfold finality of sacrifice: adoration, thanksgiving, propitiation, and the obtaining of graces. According to this fourfold finality, the sacrifice is called latreutic, eucharistic, propitiatory, and impetratory. The propitiatory and impetratory efficacies each bear a twin application, for the living and for the departed.

The conviction that the offering of the Eucharistic sacrifice can benefit the departed and obtain their everlasting happiness in the possession of God is founded on the most ancient tradition of the Church. The custom of celebrating Mass for the departed dates from at least as early as the second century. Obviously, Christians have a general awareness of their power to intercede in favor of the departed, since they pray for them; but they manifest their trust especially in the efficacy of the Eucharistic sacrifice, an efficacy which they regard as superior to that of any entreaty or prayer.

The offering of the Eucharistic sacrifice also produces an effect of grace for the living. Solidly rooted in tradition is the usage of requesting that priests offer special intentions for obtaining graces of all kinds.

The request that a priest reserve the application of the value of the Mass for a particular intention is possible not only in the case of an individual celebration, but also when there is a concelebration. Each of the concelebrants can dedicate the value of his participation to a specific intention. Even though in a concelebration we are witnessing a single sacrifice, nevertheless each concelebrant brings a participation in the act of offering, and it is in virtue of this participation that each one can apply his contribution to the value of the sacrifice for a particular intention.

Let us observe, however, that the application of the value of a Mass for a particular intention cannot absorb all of the efficacy of the Mass. The offering of the Eucharistic sacrifice produces fruits that surpass particular and expressly recalled intentions.

Actually, the fruit of every Eucharistic celebration is an ever greater development of the life of the Church. Christ is rendered present under the species of bread and wine for the sake of a broader presence in the world. We can recall the link stressed by Paul between the Eucharist and the new coming of Christ: "You proclaim the Lord's death until he comes" (1 Cor. 11:26). It is not only a matter of a link between the proclamation of the death of Christ and a coming that will signal the end of the world. After the death and resurrection of the Savior, a coming was initiated, set afoot as it were, by his glorious power manifested the day of Pentecost and enduring in the spread of the Church. In renewing the offering of the redemptive sacrifice, the Eucharist contributes to the ceaseless renewal of this coming, and thus fosters a continuous growth of the work that Christ realizes in the world through the Spirit. The words of the Eucharistic consecration bearing on the blood of the covenant poured out for the multitude are fulfilled in a real manner through the extension of the divine covenant and through the salvific power of the grace that continues to transform the whole of humanity. This fruit of the Eucharistic celebration never ceases to be produced.

It is an essential fruit, due to the supreme action of Christ, who offers the sacrifice through the act and words of the priest. This fruit is always produced, independently of the personal dispositions of the celebrant. Naturally, it is very much to be desired that the priest who celebrates the Eucharist commit himself with his whole soul in the offering of the sacrifice and conform his own attitude to that of the Savior. In doing so, he can contribute to the fecundity of the Eucharistic sacrifice for the Church and for humanity. But there is a basic fruitfulness that derives from every consecration and that guarantees spiritual enrichment to the entire Christian community. Every Mass contributes to a deeper holiness in the Church and a livelier influence of the love of the Savior upon the destiny of all human beings.

Thus, we recognize in the Eucharist a dynamism animated by the Holy Spirit, who never ceases to nourish the dynamism of the Church.

Not wrongly, then, do we assert that it is true that only the Church produces the Eucharist, but it is also true that the Eucharist produces the Church. The celebration constructs the Church, builds it up spiritually. The Eucharist, work of Christ's love in his salvific offering, develops this love in order to join Christians in a community animated by faith and by the higher life of the Savior.

Chapter 7

The Communion Meal

Value of the Meal

Intention to Institute a Banquet

At the Last Supper, Jesus' fundamental intent was to give his disciples a meal that would continue forever to nourish them in his Church. With this meal, the Savior wished to communicate the fruit of his sacrifice in the ritual realization of the sacrificial offering. He desired to give his body and blood that would be sacrificed on Calvary, but he wished to leave them as food and drink, in a meal of unique value. His aim was the institution of this meal.

In choosing bread and wine as sensible signs of the presence of his body and blood, he manifested his intention to inaugurate a meal. Not content to repeat the sacrifice, he willed that, through this meal, the fruit of his sacrifice might penetrate human life in order to transform it.

We should not be disconcerted at this intention on Christ's part. The meal is an act of social life par excellence, in which is expressed human solidarity and closeness in the life of every day. As Jesus wished to found a community animated by faith and love, it is understandable why he would have given a meal an important role in the formation and development of such a community. The Gospel accounts show us that, in public life, meals were moments at which Jesus not only maintained amicable relations with his disciples, but also sought to instruct them. In the intent of those who had invited him, they were moments at which he would formulate his doctrine or bring to light certain truths of his message. Unlike John the Baptizer, who fasted, Jesus willingly took meals with his contemporaries: "The Son of Man came eating and drinking" (Matt. 11:19). He ate and drank in order to share the life of those around him: meals were part of his numerous manifestations of love for humanity, manifestations that had become essential by reason of the mystery of the Incarnation.

The Sacred Meal

Jesus' decision to provide a spiritual meal for the development of the Church does not derive simply from the importance attaching to the meal in universal social life. In Jewish religion, the role of the meal in relations with God was not ignored. And so there were sacred meals. For example, at the striking of the covenant with God, the text of Exodus reports a twofold tradition. One describes sacrifice as an essential rite of the covenant; the other shows the expression of the covenant in the meal. As to the latter tradition, we are told that the seventy elders of Israel, who had gone up the mountain with Moses, contemplated God: "They beheld God, and they ate and drank" (Exod. 24:11). In granting them this vision, God had shown them an exceptional favor, because according to other texts it was impossible to see God without dying. Contemplation is paired with repast, which confirms the introduction into the divine intimacy. To eat and drink in someone's presence means to strike a relationship of familiarity with that person.

The sacred meal, then, acquires its value inasmuch as it opens access to the divine intimacy. For this reason, in the Old Testament the meal must be consumed in the divine abode, at the place expressly selected by God:

> You shall seek the place that the Lord your God will choose out of all your tribes as his habitation to put his name there. You shall go there, bringing there your burnt offerings and your sacrifices, your tithes and your donations, your votive gifts, your freewill offerings, and the firstlings of your herds and flocks. And you shall eat there in the presence of the Lord your God, you and your households together, rejoicing in all the undertakings in which the Lord your God has blessed you. (Deut. 12:5–7)

This description shows us the link obtaining between sacrifices and the meal. The sacrifices were to be offered in a sanctuary chosen by God, and in that same place, consecrated to God, the meals were held as well.

If the meal has the characteristic of establishing community bonds, those consummated in God's dwelling inaugurate a more profound community of life with God. On the other hand, it is God who seeks the meal, in order to strike relations of intimacy or covenant: it is God who takes the initiative. Therefore God calls the people together in a sanctuary for the organization of the meal. God is present throughout the meal. To eat is to eat in the presence of God and is therefore to develop relations of friendship with God.

The invitation to joy is characteristic of the prescriptions of the meal. "You shall rejoice before the Lord your God, you together with your sons and your daughters, your male and female slaves, and the Levites who reside in your towns" (Deut. 12:12). The invitation to joy is not only for the family, but for all those who belong to the household group, such as male and female slaves. All participate in the gladness of the meal, a gladness seen as a divine blessing.

In order to foster a more animated joy, the counsel was given to gather, at the place chosen by God, all that could be desired for a meal: "Spend the money for whatever you wish — oxen, sheep, wine, strong drink, or whatever you desire. And you shall eat there in the presence of the Lord your God, you and your household rejoicing together" (Deut. 14:26). Thus is manifested the intention of God to respond to all of the desires of those invited to the Lord's table. It is a priority of the divine love, which desires to give joy to the chosen people. Even though it imposes rules which could restrict the choice of food and attests a diffidence with regard to intoxicating drink, in the profusion of a very special meal God wishes to reveal the most fundamental divine design, which is to make the human being happy. Such meals are celebrated as banquets: religious festivals are marked by banquets, in which God is shown to be the most generous being because God secures the greatest joy.

The Eschatological Banquet

In the later part of the Book of Isaiah, called the "Apocalypse," the felicity God reserves for humanity is depicted as a sumptuous banquet. The table is set on the hill in Zion, but is prepared for "all the peoples" who will benefit from the glorious lot assigned to the Hebrew people.

> On this mountain the Lord of hosts will make for all peoples
>   a feast of rich food, a feast of well-aged wines,
> of rich food filled with marrow, of well-aged wines strained
>   clear.
> And he will destroy on this mountain
>   the shroud that is cast over all peoples,
>   the sheet that is spread over all nations;
>   he will swallow up death forever.
> Then the Lord God will wipe away the tears from all faces,
>   and the disgrace of his people he will take away from all
>   the earth,
>   for the Lord has spoken.
> It will be said on that day,
>   Lo, this is our God; we have waited for him, so that he
>   might save us.
>   This is the Lord for whom we have waited;
>   let us be glad and rejoice in his salvation. (Isa. 25:6–9)

The magnificence of the feast is amply emphasized, and a comment accompanies its description in order to make more evident the elimination of suffering and the gift of gladness. Thus does God respond to the people's divine hope.

In the Book of Consolation, the gratuity of the repast is even more clearly in evidence:

> Ho, everyone who thirsts, come to the waters;
> and you that have no money,
>   come, buy and eat!
> Come, buy wine and milk
>   without money and without price.
> Why do you spend your money for that which is not bread,
>   and your labor for that which does not satisfy?
> Listen carefully to me, and eat what is good,
>   and delight yourselves in rich food.
> Incline your ear, and come to me;
>   listen, so that you may live.

I will make with you an everlasting covenant,
   my steadfast, sure love for David. (Isa. 55: 1–3)

To the first repast, which in days of yore had ratified the covenant with Moses and the elders of Israel, corresponds the last meal,
which will signal the striking of the everlasting covenant in faithfulness to the promises made to David. The meal explains all of
the benefits, all of the graces that God will give human beings with
this covenant.

In the Book of the Parables of Enoch, as well, which is chronologically nearer to the time of Christ, the felicity of the life to come
is presented in the image of a heavenly banquet. "The Lord of
spirits will abide with them, and they shall eat with the Son of
Man. They will take part in his table for everlasting ages" (62:14).
Happiness, then, will consist in finding oneself at table with the
Messiah, or Son of Man, very close to the Lord of spirits, that is,
God. The promise of everlasting felicity is based especially on this
company.

The Spiritual Meal

In the proclamation of the heavenly banquet, the accent of certain
apocalyptic predictions had been placed on the excellence of the
fare, in order to show the divine generosity. Another current of
thought drew attention especially to the divine Wisdom. The Book
of Proverbs describes the banquet offered to all by Wisdom:

Wisdom has built her house,
   she has hewn her seven pillars.
She has slaughtered her animals, she has mixed her wine,
   she has also set her table.
She has sent out her servant girls, she calls
   from the highest places in the town,
"You that are simple, turn in here!"
   To those without sense she says,
"Come, eat of my bread
   and drink of the wine I have mixed.
Lay aside immaturity, and live,
   and walk in the way of insight." (Prov. 9:1–6)

The invitation to eat the bread and drink the wine of Wisdom therefore represents an invitation to receive this wisdom in one's own mind and in one's own life. It is a matter of abandoning foolishness to find true life and of conducting oneself in the most just manner. The invitation is particularly addressed to the simplest, that is, to those who could not think that they already had wisdom. The gift of the divine Wisdom is offered to those who are a target for scorn, because the generosity of the divine love seeks to be poured out especially on the poor and the little.

In the book of Sirach, the divine Wisdom is presented as the source of benefits that promise abundant, inebriating meals:

> Wisdom intoxicates with her fruits the devout themselves.
> Their whole house she will fill with desirable things, their storehouses with her fruits. (Sir. 1:16b–17)

But she does not limit herself to pouring out her fruits in abundance: she offers herself as food and drink:

> Come to me, you who desire me, and fill yourselves from my largess.
> For my memory is sweeter than honey, and possessing me is sweeter than the honeycomb. Those who feed on me will hunger again, and those who drink of me will thirst again.
> (Sir. 24:18–20)

In the words addressed to Jesus by the Samaritan woman there is a complement of what the Old Testament had announced through the banquet of Wisdom. Besides, this complement of the figures of the old covenant is verified in the Eucharist, where Jesus, like Wisdom of old, offers himself as food and drink.

The Eucharistic Meal

Incarnation and Repast

The announcement of the banquet of Wisdom in the old covenant was actually orientated toward the Eucharist, since the personage of Wisdom finds in Jesus her complement. Jesus actually identified himself with Wisdom when he asserted, "Wisdom is vindicated by her deeds" (Matt. 11:19). The deeds of Wisdom consisted in the miracles performed by Jesus and all of his salvific activity.

Jesus realizes in the most concrete way what Wisdom had desired in the banquet to be set: to be eaten, to be drunk. Wisdom's assertions could have only a metaphorical value: When Wisdom said, "Those who feed on me,... those who drink of me," the only meaning the verse to "eat" and to "drink" could have was a symbolic one. In the proper sense, it was impossible to eat or drink Wisdom. One could only seek for Wisdom in the sense of thinking and acting and of receiving it as a divine gift that transforms one's mentality.

Instead, in Jesus' case, the acts of eating and drinking preserve their meaning and value, as the words make abundantly clear in the discourse that promises the institution of the Eucharist: "Those who eat my flesh and drink my blood have eternal life" (John 6:54). Of course, what is given to eat and to drink is not ordinary food or drink. One eats the flesh of Christ in his glorious state, a flesh henceforth filled with the Holy Spirit: one drinks his blood in the same state. But eating and drinking are essential: "For my flesh is true food and my blood is true drink" (John 6:55). While taking on a new meaning in the mystery of the presence of the body and blood of Christ, the meal consists in eating and drinking.

What makes this eating and drinking possible is the primordial mystery of the Incarnation. Wisdom had been described as a divine person come among human beings, but who had not become incarnate. It had neither flesh nor blood. Jesus, on the other hand, is the divine person come into the world with the full reality of an incarnation that makes him live like other human beings, in a condition of flesh and blood.

In virtue of the Incarnation, Jesus defines himself as Eucharistic bread: "I am the bread of life" (John 6:35). This expression, used in the Gospel of John, affords a glimpse of the fact that the divine person of Christ is itself the nourishment given to humanity for a new life. The divine person is the bread of life only through the body and blood that belong to him. Still, it remains true that it is the Son of God as a person who offers himself as food and drink.

Jesus insists on this involvement of his divine person of the Son in the Eucharistic meal when he asserts: "The bread of God is that which comes down from heaven and gives life to the world" (John 6:33). The divine gift of the bread coincides with the gift of the Incarnation: it is the word "bread" that gives us to recognize the Eucharist in his announcement. In the Eucharistic consecration, the Son comes down from heaven and, in the Eucharistic meal, gives life to the world. In this fashion, the Eucharist never ceases to renew the process of the Incarnation. The bread of God is not simply the bread given by God; in terms of the assertion "I am," it is actually God who is offered as bread. In the Eucharist, Jesus involves not only his body and blood, but his whole self. Thus, the Eucharistic meal consists in his communicating his own life to human beings. It is a matter of communication of the divine life itself, the life possessed by the Son and placed at the disposition of all who are destined to share his Sonship. This is all contained in the declaration, "Those who eat my flesh and drink my blood have eternal life" (John 6:54).

The entire life of grace is the communication of this eternal life of the Son. But the communication occurs par excellence in the Eucharist. The act of eating and drinking represents a deeper penetration of Christ's life into the interior of the individual, a more complete assimilation of one's personal life to the higher life of the incarnate Son.

Banquet Animated by the Life-giving Spirit

The Old Testament had proclaimed a spiritual banquet, the one offered by Wisdom, in which divine Wisdom gave itself as food and drink. This proclamation is fulfilled thanks to the fact that Jesus as a divine person offers himself as food and drink with his body and blood.

But the spiritual banquet, according to the elucidations given in the Gospels, involves an essential contribution on the part of the Holy Spirit. Jesus vigorously reacted to the incomprehension of the audience, who had thought that the Eucharistic food was that of his flesh in its present, earthly state. We have already commented on the reply in which Jesus underscores that the flesh given as food will be that of the Son of Man returned to heaven, that is, a flesh animated by the Holy Spirit, since in itself, in its sole quality as flesh, "the flesh is useless" (John 6:63). "It is the spirit that gives life" (John 6:63). Jesus shows us in what sense all of the words bearing on the flesh and blood of the Son of Man are to be understood: they are words that are "Spirit and life." This flesh and this blood are realties in which the life of the Spirit is found, the life that confers on them their full meaning.

When we assert that in the Eucharistic meal Jesus communicates his own divine life, since it is he who is eaten and drunk, we must therefore specify that this life is given through the Holy Spirit. Even as Eucharistic food and drink, Christ works, and transforms humanity, through the Spirit. At Pentecost, at the moment of bringing the Church to birth, it is he who, according to Peter's discourse, pours forth the Holy Spirit that he has received from the Father (Acts 2:33). This first emergence of the Christian community contained the principle and source of its entire future development, in which the Holy Spirit would discharge an essential role.

In conformity with this principle of the development of the saving and transforming activity of Christ through the Holy Spirit, the Eucharist implies, in flesh given as food, a special animation due to the Spirit. The Eucharistic meal propagates the life of the Spirit. This does not mean that the Eucharist is to be considered a sacrament of the Holy Spirit. It remains food and drink that consist in the body and blood of Christ. It is the task of the Holy Spirit to glorify Christ (John 15:14), and when the power of the Spirit produces witnesses, they are witnesses of Christ (Acts 1:8). It is always Christ, then, who offers himself as food and drink, but the food and the drink receive their spiritual efficacy from the Holy Spirit, who fills them to overflowing.

Through the Eucharistic banquet, then, the gifts of the Holy Spirit are poured forth among Christians. In the First Letter to the Corinthians (12:1–11), Saint Paul describes the diversity of the spiritual gifts, or charisms, that characterize the life and growth of the Church. They are gifts distributed in a general manner, according to the sovereign will of the Holy Spirit; there is no reference to the Eucharist. Nevertheless, when Paul subsequently enjoins Christians to aspire to the higher gifts, faith, hope, and especially charity (see 1 Cor. 12:31, 13:13), we must not forget that, in the acquisition of these gifts, the Eucharist can have an important role.

In an altogether special way in the case of charity, the role of the Eucharist must certainly not be forgotten. Indeed, Jesus has shown the link between the Eucharist and charity when, at the Last Supper, he formulated the new commandment: "Love one another as I have loved you" (John 15:12; see 13:34). To disciples who had too often expressed their rivalry, he granted with the Eucharist the spiritual strength necessary to maintain relationships of charity and understanding. He relied on the Eucharistic banquet to make his disciples capable of observing the great precept of mutual love. The divine gift contained in this meal, the gift of the victory of love over all contrary passions, was a gift of the Holy Spirit.

Granted, the Eucharist is not the only channel of the gifts of the Holy Spirit. But it is an important one, especially for the diffusion of charity. In giving himself as spiritual food, Jesus kindles in all human hearts the fire of love through the Holy Spirit.

Eucharist and Epiclesis

Since the Holy Spirit performs a life-giving role in the gift of the body and blood of Christ given as food and drink, we are not surprised that that Spirit would have a special role in the offering of the sacrifice and in the spiritual fruit of the meal. That role is expressed in the liturgy through the epiclesis.

The epiclesis is the invocation whose purpose it is to obtain the gift of the Holy Spirit. The epiclesis bears especially on the consecration: the Holy Spirit is invoked for the purpose of the transformation of the bread and wine into the body and blood of Christ. There is also an epiclesis whose objective is communion: the spiritual effect of the Eucharistic banquet is besought of the Holy Spirit.

In the matter of the epiclesis, whose reference is to the consecration, there is disagreement between Orthodox and Catholics, inasmuch as the Orthodox regard the epiclesis as the essential formula whose effect is the consecration. In this perspective, the words of institution would only express what is effectuated by the epiclesis. At the Council of Florence, the Decree for the Armenians asserts that the form of the sacrament consists in the words of the Savior, the words of institution (DS 1321). Many pontifical assertions regard as necessary and sufficient for the validity of the consecration the words of Christ. Pius X says clearly: "Cath-

olic doctrine on the sacrament of the Holy Eucharist is not free
from discussion: it is obstinately taught that we may accept the
opinion according to which, with the Greeks, the words of consecration obtain their purpose only after the recital of the invocation
of the epiclesis" (DS 3556). The Holy Office, on May 23, 1957,
declared that one validly celebrates who pronounces the words of
consecration.[20]

From this we cannot conclude, however, that the epiclesis is
without value. The descent of the Holy Spirit is besought in the
Eucharistic celebration because that descent corresponds to the accomplishment of the Eucharistic mystery: it is through the Holy
Spirit that Christ's offering rises to the Father, and it is through
the Holy Spirit that the bread and wine, in this offering, are
transformed into the body and blood of Christ.

---

20. *AAS* 49 (1957), 370.

Chapter 8

Worship of
the Eucharistic Presence

Development of the Worship of the Real Presence

The Eucharistic presence, on the basis of Christ's twice stated command "Do this in remembrance of me" (1 Cor. 11:24–25, Luke 22:19), is at the root of a considerable liturgical development, which has broadened in the course of the centuries. Around the core of the double consecration, prayers, rites, and readings have taken shape with which the Christian community makes an effort to share as intensively as possible in the memorial instituted by the Savior.

More particularly, it is important to note a relatively late development bearing on a devotion to the Eucharistic presence. In the early centuries, the Eucharist was publicly adored, but only during the time of the Mass and Communion. The reservation of the consecrated host was originally for the purpose of bringing Communion to the sick and the absent. Only during the Middle Ages, in the West, did there arise a more explicit worship of the real presence, with the emphasis on adoration.

In the twelfth century, a new rite was introduced into the celebration of the Mass: the elevation of the consecrated host immediately after the consecration. This elevation constitutes an invitation to acknowledge more expressly the presence of Christ and to adore him.

In the thirteenth century, the adoration of the host developed outside of the Mass, along with popular attendance at processions of the Most Holy Sacrament.

At the instigation of Saint Julian of Mont Cornillon, in Liege, Belgium, in 1247, the Feast of the Most Holy Sacrament was introduced. With the bull *Transiturus*, in 1264, Pope Urban IV extended the feast to the universal Church: the Feast of Corpus Christi, instituted in order to "adore, venerate, glorify, love, and embrace" this so exalted sacrament.

In the fourteenth century, the usage of the exposition of the host in the monstrance was introduced. Subsequently, in certain regions, the Most Holy Sacrament was exposed during the recital of the canonical hours. Blessings with the sacrament multiplied. At the end of the fifteenth century, the Forty Hours Adoration of the Blessed Sacrament exposed came into use, in commemoration of the forty hours spent by our Lord in the tomb.

During the Renaissance, a tabernacle was erected on the main altar. Private visits to the Blessed Sacrament spread in the eighteenth century under the influence of Saint Alphonsus Maria de Liguori.

We cannot fail to recognize in all of this development a doctrinal value: what we have is an evolution founded on faith in the Eucharistic presence of Christ. It is worthy of note that the Office of Corpus Domini was anticipated by Saint Thomas Aquinas: a sign that the institution of the feast was in harmony with theological reflection. Let us recall the poetic words that the Saint wrote for the occasion: the "Pange Lingua":

> Sing, my tongue, the Savior's glory,
> of his flesh the mystery sing,
> and of his precious blood,
> given in price for the world,
> fruit of the noble womb.

> Given to us by a mother pure,
> for us all he became incarnate.
> His fecund word
> he sowed amid the nations,
> and with a generous love
> consummated his life.

> In the night of the Last Supper,
> reclining with his brethren,
> having fulfilled to the letter
> the sacred rite of Passover,

he gave himself as food
to the astonished Apostles.

The word of the Lord
transformed bread and wine:
bread into flesh, wine into blood
he consecrated for a memorial.
Not the senses, but faith
proves this truth.

Let us adore the sacrament
that God the Father gave us.
A new covenant, a new rite,
was accomplished in faith.
The foundation of the mystery
are the words of Jesus.

Glory to the almighty Father,
glory to the Son, the Redeemer,
great praise and highest honor
to eternal Charity!
Glory immense, eternal love
to the Holy Trinity!
Amen.

The Council of Trent, after having proclaimed the real presence
and the transubstantiation, enunciates the fundamental principle of
the worship of adoration due to the Eucharist:

Thus, there is no reason to doubt that all of the faithful, according to the usage always received in the Catholic Church,
ought to render, in veneration of the Most Holy Sacrament,
the worship of latria due to the true God. Indeed, the fact
that it was instituted by Christ our Lord as food does not
militate against its adoration. We believe that, in it, that same
God is present of whom the eternal Father has said, introducing him into the world, "All gods bow down before him" (Ps.
97:7); the Magi "knelt down and paid him homage" (Matt.
2:11); and finally Scripture attests that he was "worshiped"
in Galilee by his Apostles (Matt. 28:17). (DS 1643)

Worship of the Real Presence in the Eucharistic Celebration

It will be in order to recall that, at the moment of the institution of the Eucharist, Jesus stated directly and immediately that his body and blood were present. Since he was inviting his disciples to eat and drink, he could have said only: "Eat my body," and "Drink my blood." But he preferred to make use of words proclaiming the reality of his flesh and blood: "This [is] my body," and "This [is] my blood."

He asked his disciples to believe in this reality. Hence, a year before the Last Supper, he had required an act of faith on the part of his disciples, an act of faith all the more meritorious and more valid inasmuch as it represented a resistance to the general movement of defection that had occurred at the moment of the proclamation of the Eucharist. Jesus had required that act of faith as the condition to be accepted in order to continue to follow him: "Do you also wish to go away?" he asked the Twelve.

In order to remain with the Master, the disciples must believe in the mysterious meal in which the Son of Man would give his flesh to eat and his blood to drink. They must acknowledge in him the bread come down from heaven, the bread that gives life to the world. The act of faith required of the disciples is before all else an act of faith in the divine person of Christ. Only one who is God can secure life for the world by making himself the nourishment of human beings. Peter, overcome, confesses this: "Lord, to whom can we go? You have the words of eternal life" (John 6:68). To whom indeed, if not to the one who pronounces divine words and possesses the holiness of God.

In the Eucharist, there is an essential assertion of the divine presence. Thus, there is an invitation to adoration. The one who, in his body and blood, offers himself as food and drink asks to be received in function of the divine value of his gift.

Jesus' declarations regarding his personal presence in the Eucharist must be accepted in all of their implications. These implications go beyond the declaration that his flesh is given as food and his blood as drink, since the presence of a person cannot be reduced to the utility it presents or the service it renders. Even when Jesus says, "Whoever eats me...," he alludes to a personal presence that is not exhausted in a function of nourishment.

The Eucharistic presence can never be regarded as the presence of a thing, constituted of body and blood. It is essentially the presence of the one who, through his body and blood, says: "I am." This presence deserves to be appreciated in function of the dignity of a person become present with love and, more precisely, with the supreme dignity of a divine person.

Therefore, in the sharing of the Eucharistic celebration, an attitude of adoration before Jesus who has become present precedes the Communion meal. Only this adoration can afford the Christian the dispositions for receiving the body and blood of Jesus with the respect and veneration that are due to them. Only this adoration can give Communion its true meaning, that of an intimate contact, person to person, with the Son of God made man.

Let us specify the sense of the adoration here. We could wonder, indeed, whether adoration could be addressed to a wafer. The adoration goes further than the wafer as such, which now is but a sensible sign of the presence of the body of Christ. This body can and should be adored, because it belongs to the divine person of the Son of God. Actually, the adoration is addressed solely to the person. This is recalled in profound words by the ancient hymn "Adoro Te Devote":

Hidden God, devoutly I adore you,
who under these figures are hidden, but true.
To you my heart submits altogether,
for, contemplating you, it fails altogether.

Vision, touch, taste, fail to reach you.
But hearing — hearing your words — is to be believed.
I believe whatever God's Son has said:
nothing is truer than this Word of all truth.

On the Cross, you have hidden your divinity.
Here on the altar you also veil your humanity.
O human being and God, faith reveals you to me:
just as to the good thief, give me heaven one day.

Though you do not give me to touch your wounds,
with Thomas I cry, "You are my Lord!"
May faith grow in me, I wish to hope in you,
my heart has found rest only in your love.

You are the eternal memory that the Lord has died.
Living bread, life, are what you become for me.
Let my mind have light from you,
and inwardly taste your manna.

Like the pelican, you nourish us with yourself.
Sunk in sin I cry, "Wash me, Lord!"
Your blood is fire: burn away our error.
One single drop has the power to save all.

Now I gaze upon the host, where you are hidden:
I burn with thirst to see you.
When this flesh shall dissolve,
your vision, O light, will reveal itself.
Amen.

Worship of the Real Presence outside the Eucharistic Celebration

Jesus did not expressly ask that worship of his Eucharistic Presence be paid outside the celebration of the Eucharistic sacrifice and Communion. But by the words of consecration, he has given us the presence of his body and blood, with an assertion that placed no limits on this presence.

True, he has given his body and blood in the accomplishment of the offering of the sacrifice that sacramentally reproduces the sacrifice of the Cross, and it is through the offering of the Cross that his personal presence is bestowed in the Eucharist. But he has not closed up this presence in the space and time needed for the offering of the Eucharistic sacrifice.

In like manner, bestowing his presence under the signs of bread and wine, he was thinking of the Communion meal. But he certainly did not express a will that the gift of his body and blood should cease once the meal had come to an end.

We need only recall that the words of consecration, carefully selected by Jesus, while including an invitation to eat and drink, are limited to an assertion of the reality of the body and blood without an indication of any limit in time for their presence. Hence, as long as the "species" last without corrupting, the presence of the body and blood remains unchanged.

Furthermore, let us stress that the words "This [is] my body" and "This [is] my blood" express a gift made to human beings. We could translate, "Behold my body,... behold my blood." As it comes from Jesus, this is a gift of a generosity without limits. With these most simple words, he has left in the hands of his disciples his sacramental presence. He has not sought to place restrictions on the duration of this presence, leaving to his Church the concern of receiving it in all the breadth of the divine gift that this presence involves. Let us say, then, that, in the intention of Christ, the Eucharistic presence is a completely open gift, without any restrictions.

True, the Eucharistic presence remains a gift essentially destined for the celebration of the Eucharistic sacrifice and the Communion meal. It can never be considered or venerated apart from all realization in the celebration. The adoration of the real presence prepares for the offering of the sacrifice and for Communion. Besides, it derives its validity from the sacrifice and the meal, after that sacrifice and that meal have been celebrated. That is, it is simultaneously an introduction to the celebration, and a fruit of the same.

Christ's intent to develop the worship of his presence is more particularly discovered in the promise made to the disciples before his definitive departure from the earth: "I am with you always, to the end of the age" (Matt. 28:20). This promise, which concludes the Gospel of Matthew, is of a unique value. It makes allusion to the name of God already cited in Matthew 1:23: Emmanuel, "God with us." This name manifests the Master's essential concern in the moment he is about to withdraw from his disciples' view. Knowing that he is about to cause them the sorrow of his absence, he guarantees a continuous presence. And he adds the specification "with you" to assure them that it is a matter of a presence of which they can never be deprived: henceforth they are indissolubly united to the person of Christ. Then he specifies that his presence will endure "always," as a presence that will sign the ordinary course of all of their days. In saying that it will be thus "to the end of the age," Jesus affords his disciples a glimpse of the fact that his presence will accompany them in the great mission of evangelization of all the nations, which will come to an end only with the conclusion of the history of humanity.

If Jesus had the intention of guaranteeing this presence in virtue of the continuous intimate relationship he sought to establish with his disciples, then we cannot escape the conclusion that he desired to offer them the presence which he himself had placed at their disposition through the institution of the Eucharist. Since the intimacy into which he had entered with human beings had a sacramental aspect, the presence with which he desired to favor them must have a sacramental aspect also, and this must be realized through the Eucharist. This so intimate presence to everyone, a daily presence, guaranteed to the end of the age, is most adequately realized through the Eucharist.

At the Last Supper, pronouncing the words of consecration for the first time, Jesus was not unaware of the fact that the presence of his body and blood was destined to transform the destiny of humanity. Can we not think that he had the interior certitude that his flesh would be acknowledged as the ideal nourishment by all who hunger for God? Besides, conscious as he was of drawing all human beings to himself (see John 12:32), he desired to become, through the Eucharist, the center of adoration for all believers, offering to those who would adhere to him a more tranquil opportunity for worship and contemplative intimacy.

Central Role of the Real Presence

In the course of the centuries, the development of worship of the real presence has represented a progress in consciousness of the wealth of the mystery of the Eucharist.

This worship fully harmonizes with the celebration of the sacrifice and of the Eucharistic meal. It contributes to a better grasp of the sense of participation in the sacramental offering of Christ. It tends to concentrate greater attention on the person of the Savior in Communion.

In some of the manifestations of worship, we cannot fail to recognize a thrust of intense veneration with which the people seek to attest their gratitude for the divine gift of the Eucharist. But we should add that Christ himself had desired this response at the institution performed at the Last Supper and had wished to awaken a movement of adoration which would acknowledge the value of his presence.

This presence is an appeal to faith and love. It occupies a central position in the Christian religion, as a presence bound to the new temple built by the Resurrection. It is a wellspring of hope, given that the Eucharist associates us to the Passion of Christ "until he comes" (1 Cor. 11:26).

Eucharistic Worship in the Eastern Churches

There has never been a Eucharistic worship in the Eastern Churches because there have not been the historical conditions there that have impelled the Latin Church to intensify its worship of the real presence of Christ in the Eucharist not only during the Eucharistic celebration but also apart from it. Every tradition of the Church has the right to express itself according to its own inspiration, its own rites, and its own customs. Indeed, as the Conciliar Decree on the Eastern Catholic Churches sets forth, among the various rites of the Church "there flourishes such an admirable brotherhood that this variety within the Church in no way harms her unity, but rather manifests it. For it is the mind of the Catholic Church that each individual Church or rite retain its traditions whole and entire" (Vatican II, *Orientalium Ecclesiarum*, no. 2). We must likewise keep in mind that, as the same Second Vatican Council asserts, all of the rites of the Church, all of their traditions, all of their spiritual legacies, "enjoy the same rights and are under the same obligations" (ibid., no. 3).

Nevertheless, while there does not exist a tradition of Eucharistic worship in the Eastern Churches apart from the Mass (holy hour, benediction, Eucharistic processions, and so on), these churches (both those in communion with the Bishop of Rome and those not in full communion) nevertheless cultivate a great veneration for the Holy Eucharist even outside the celebration of the sacred liturgy.

By tradition, these Churches are more inclined to pay external worship especially to the sacred icons, regarded as a "sacramental" of personal presence. In these is represented a face (especially the face of Christ) or events in the history of salvation (especially the mysteries of Christ and of the Mother of God) which, in concomitance with the Eucharistic celebration and in strict accord with it and the liturgical year, render present for the faithful the mystery being celebrated and incline believers to imitate the prototype. Here the Seventh Ecumenical Council (Nicaea II, on sacred images) teaches:

> The more frequently these images are contemplated, so much the more are those who contemplate them referred to the memory and desire of the original models, and inspired to attribute to them, by kissing them, respect and veneration.... The honor paid to the image actually belongs to the one who is represented there, and the one who venerates the image venerates the reality of the one reproduced in it.
>
> (Mansi, 13:482)

The Eucharist can be regarded as the icon par excellence, as it is the sacrament of the one who is the "image [*eikona*] of the invisible God" (Col. 1:15).

The division prevailing among Christians is a source of great suffering, because it is an obstacle to a common participation in the Eucharist, that "center and summit" of the life of the Church and sacrament of unity.

Indeed, the Eucharist at once expresses unity and communicates grace. As an expression of unity, *communicatio in sacris* is impossible. As a means of grace, it can be permitted in precise circumstances determined by the authority of the Church (see Vatican II, *Unitatis Redintegratio*, no. 8).

As for the Eastern Orthodox Churches, these have true sacraments, principally in virtue of the apostolic succession. Thus, *communicatio in sacris* is not only permitted in certain circumstances, but positively recommended, in conformity with the directives of ecclesiastical authority (see ibid., no. 15).

According to Catholic doctrine, the Churches and communities of the Protestant tradition have not preserved the genuine and integral substance of the Eucharistic mystery. A common participation in the Eucharist, then, is impossible. The sacraments and their ministers must be a subject for dialogue (see ibid., no. 22). Indeed, significant steps toward unity have already been taken. The participation of all Christians at the one table of the Lord should be the object of our intense prayers.

The Eucharistic Congress

Introducing Christians into the third millennium of their history as it does, the jubilee of the year 2000 inspires them to contemplate, with ever new eyes, the mystery of the Incarnation of God. In Jesus of Nazareth, God became a human being in order to reveal the Trinitarian mystery of the divine love and to save humanity. As we have seen above, this mystery extends through history, and human beings in every age have asked themselves how it is possible for God to love so intensely as to give over the divinity in the supreme act of death on a cross. This event does not regard only a fact of the past, but, through the mediation of the sacrament of the Eucharist, is activated every day, to the end of the ages. Indeed, it attests that Jesus is with us forever, and loves us, offering the forgiveness of reconciliation and communion of life with God.

It is a fact charged with meaning, therefore, that John Paul II should have wished to have the celebration of the International Eucharistic Congress during the course of the Great Jubilee. In the letter *Tertio Millennio Adveniente* he writes:

> Christ being the sole access to the Father, in order to emphasize his living and salvific presence in the Church and on earth, there will be held at Rome, on the occasion of the Great Jubilee, the International Eucharistic Congress. The year 2000 will be an intensely Eucharistic year: in the sacrament of the Eucharist, the Savior, having become incarnate in

Mary's womb twenty centuries ago, continues to offer himself to humanity as source of divine life. (No. 55)

Therefore the Holy Year has its heart and its crowning moment in the International Eucharistic Congress, since the celebration of the Eucharistic mystery is the center of the entire life of the Church. They will not be two events, then, but each will be celebrated in the light of the other, one single event full of meaning.

The celebration of the International Eucharistic Congress will take place, temporally as well, in the middle of the Year of Jubilee, and in the city in which Peter and Paul gave Christ the supreme witness of their love. Opening before us are the gates of a new millennium of the Christian era: the Eucharistic Congress becomes a call for a more consistent testimonial of faith, in order to respond with conviction to the various needs present in the heart of each person. The Church of Rome, convoked by its bishop, the Pope, well knows the peculiar mission characterizing it before its sister churches. In celebrating this Eucharistic Congress, it will have to express once more its faithfulness to the mission that, by a providential, utterly hidden divine design, Christ has willed to be entrusted only to it.

Accordingly, Christians are called precisely to celebrate this Eucharistic Congress, as an event from which to draw new strength to be able to correspond always to their mission through a new evangelization. Pilgrims in the Year of Jubilee should be able to gather the riches of the grace that the Eucharist offers and will be able to open their hearts to a great hope by their expectation of the return of the Risen Lord.

Chapter 9

The Eucharist in the Life of Christians

Intimate Union with Christ

The first effect of the Eucharistic meal is a more intimate union with Jesus. He enters as food into the persons of the faithful, to establish the deepest bonds with them, and transform their whole inner lives.

Jesus declares: "Those who eat my flesh and drink my blood abide in me, and I in them" (John 6:56). Thus, the purpose of the Eucharistic meal consists not in a temporary union, but in a lasting one. The one who receives the body of Christ in Communion receives it to create an intimacy destined to be prolonged.

Speaking of the life of grace at the Last Supper, Jesus defines himself as a vine, whose branches propagate life. The challenge for the branches is to remain attached to the vine. "Abide in me, as I in you," Jesus says. The first effect of compliance with this request and warning is to ensure the fertility of life: "Just as the branch cannot bear fruit by itself unless it abides in the vine, neither can you unless you abide in me" (John 15:4). "Those who abide in me and I in them bear much fruit, because apart from me you can do nothing" (John 15:5). But fertility is not the only aim, important as it is. To "abide" united to Christ, to remain in him as he dwells in us, is an objective to be pursued for its own sake, since it corresponds to a person's most profound need. Saint Paul's example shows that we are dealing with the most fundamental aspiration of the human being, at least of that human being who has discovered Christ and who believes in him. Paul expressed his desire for happiness in the next world as follows: "My desire is to depart and be with Christ" (Phil. 1:23).

The Eucharist can respond to this aspiration in the present life. The Eucharistic meal is a meal of Communion with Christ — that is, a meal that establishes a union with him, one that involves the whole being and enables the believer to remain in him as he abides in us.

The Presence of Mary in the Community That Celebrates the Eucharist

Experience of the Church as Eucharistic and Marian

The Eucharist is the soul of the Church. It is the living heart of great cathedrals as it is of small, poor mission chapels. But alongside the Eucharist the piety of the faithful always places the image of the Blessed Virgin. The reason is that Mary is seen as associated to Christ her Son in the community that celebrates the Eucharist. She makes essential, continuous reference to the Eucharistic Christ, as if she were seeking to stress the need for the spiritual nourishment and communion afforded by the sacrament of the Eucharist. The Blessed Virgin seems to have a charismatic ministry as guide of the faithful to the Eucharist. This is what occurs on Marian pilgrimages and in Marian sanctuaries, where everything is centered on the Eucharist, the source and crown of all Marian piety and spirituality.

Biblical Foundations

Is this a "Catholic peculiarity," or does this presence of Mary in the community that celebrates the Eucharist have a biblical foundation?

At first sight, it would seem that there are only indirect indications of this theme. There are passages, for example, in which we find allusions to the participation of the first Christian community in the Lord's Supper (1 Cor. 11:16–20) or at the breaking of the bread (Acts 2:42–47, 20:7). Very probably Mary was part of the community life, participating in the Eucharist presided over by the Apostles.

There is also the question of whether Mary was present at the Last Supper. The answer is that her presence cannot be excluded, for two reasons: (1) According to John 19:27, Mary was in Jerusalem precisely during those days. (2) According to Jewish usage at the Passover supper, it fell to the mother of the family — as is still true today — to light the lamps: it may be, then, that it was Mary who performed this duty at the Last Supper.

Finally, as Luke emphasizes, there is the decidedly Eucharistic symbolic value of the name "Bethlehem," which, according to a popular etymology, would mean "house of bread" (as Mary is the "house" par excellence of the bread of life that is Christ), and of the manger in which the infant was placed (Luke 2:7, 12, 16).

But there are other data, much more meaningful and pertinent, furnished us by John in two scenes highly symbolic, from the Eucharistic standpoint, in which Mary has a central role at Jesus' side. We refer to the episode of the wedding at Cana (John 2), to be understood in strict parallel with that of the multiplication of the loaves in John 6 and the episode on Calvary in John 19.

The initiation of the sign of the wine is decidedly that of Mary, with the order given to the servants, "Do whatever he tells you" (John 2:5). Cana is the beginning of the signs, including the sign of bread, and represents the beginning of a new sacramental "economy," of which the center is the Eucharist.

In this new economy, Mary is called not "mother," but rather "woman." This passage indicates that the Blessed Virgin becomes "family founder" (that is, "woman," Gen. 2:23) of a new generation, that of the Church community, which is nourished by the Eucharistic blood and body of Christ. John the Evangelist here stresses the role of the Virgin Mother in the post-Easter Church community.

Not only in the book of signs, but also in that of the Passion, John makes a decisive contribution to the Eucharistic dimension of the figure of Mary. In John 19:25–27, Jesus entrusts the disciple to Mary and Mary to the disciple. This is not only an act of filial piety on the part of Jesus, but also an episode of definitive revelation. Mary becomes the vessel of a mysterious motherhood. Here too she is called "woman," once more in order to underscore the beginning in her of a new generation, that of the Church, which springs from the pierced side of Christ, from which flowed blood and water, symbol of the sacraments of the Church.

In the new sacramental economy, inaugurated by the Church that is the salvific presence of Christ in history, Mary remains mother. If at first she was only the mother of the Son, now she is also the mother of the Church. If at first her motherhood was physical, now it is spiritual, as well. On Calvary, the mother of Jesus becomes the mother of the disciples.

Mary's physical motherhood seems destroyed, as it were, not only in words, but in a terribly realistic manner: with the physical death of her Son. A spiritual motherhood succeeds it: Mary becomes the mother of the disciple. While at first it had been Jesus who was born of the Virgin, now it is the Virgin who receives a new birth from her crucified Son. Jesus no longer calls her "mother," but "woman," because she is taken from man (see Gen. 2:23). It is difficult to imagine a more radical change of relationship between Mary and her divine Son.

In the place of Jerusalem, the "daughter of Zion," mother of the scattered whom God reunites within her walls and in her Temple, comes Mary, mother of the scattered children reunited by Jesus in the temple of the new covenant, which is his body and his blood poured out for all for a remission of sins. In the economy of the new covenant, Mary becomes the personification of the new Jerusalem, the Church animated sacramentally by the Eucharistic Christ.

Mary, then, has a presence and a decisive role both in the Incarnation and in the sacramental economy of the Church. In both cases she has said her "fiat," in faith, in hope, in charity. In both, she is the founder of a new generation according to the will of God: in the first, the generation of the Son of God made flesh; in the second, the generation of the Church community that springs from the side of Christ, nourished by his body and blood.

The Church, sacrament of salvation, besides being essentially Eucharistic, also has an existential Marian character.

Mary Leads to the Eucharist

Therefore the Church never celebrates the Eucharist without repeatedly invoking the intercession of the Mother of the Lord. At each Mass, Mary offers as most exalted member of the Church not only her past consent to the Incarnation and the Cross, but also her merits and her present glorious motherly intercession (see *Marialis Cultus*, no. 20).

John Paul II's encyclical *Redemptoris Mater* declares that Mary's spiritual motherhood "is particularly sensed and lived by the Christian people in the Sacred Repast — the liturgical celebration of the mystery of redemption — in which Christ, his true body born of the Virgin Mary, is made present" (no. 44). And it continues:

> With good reason has the piety of the Christian people always recognized a deep bond between devotion to the Holy Virgin and the worship of the Eucharist. This is a fact that may be gathered from the liturgy, whether Western or Eastern, from the traditions of religious families, from the spirituality of contemporary movements, including youth movements, from the pastoral practices of the Marian sanctuaries. *Mary guides the faithful to the Eucharist.* (Ibid.)

Far from divorcing the faithful from Jesus, this charismatic office of Mary guides them maternally to sacramental Communion with him, as an offering of grace for a Christian life of harmonious, strong witness.

Condition for Development of Life

The Communion meal has been instituted by Jesus as the ordinary means of development of his life in his disciples. It is not a luxury, although the gift of his body and blood is a boon of extreme generosity. It is a condition for the development of the life of grace.

Even before the miracle of the multiplication of the loaves, which announced the future Eucharist, Jesus had expressed his essential concern: "I have compassion for the crowd, because they have been with me now for three days and have nothing to eat. If I send them away hungry to their homes, they will faint on the way — and some of them have come from a great distance" (Mark 8:2–3). The bread that Jesus will give to his audience is necessary to keep them from fainting. The miracle responds to an evident need.

After the miracle, Jesus clearly formulates the necessity of the Eucharistic meal for the spiritual life: "Very truly I tell you, unless you eat the flesh of the Son of Man and drink his blood, you have no life in you" (John 6:53). It is a declaration of a solemn character, a declaration in which Jesus commits all of his doctrinal authority. He shows to what extent the Eucharist is indispensable for the Christian life: it is a condition for the possession of true life. Commenting on this passage, Byzantine theologian Nicholas Cabasilas (fourteenth century) asserts:

> In accordance with His promise we dwell in Christ by means of the feast and Christ dwells in us, for he says, "he abides in me, and I in him" (John 6:57).
> But when Christ dwells in us, what else is needed, or what benefit escapes us? When we dwell in Christ, what else will we desire? He dwells in us, and he is our dwelling place. How blessed are we by reason of this dwelling place!...
> ...It is not some ray of light which we receive in our souls, but the very orb of the sun. So we dwell in him and are indwelt and become one spirit with him.

What is the result? The more excellent things overcome the inferior, things divine prevail over the human, and what Paul says concerning the Resurrection takes place: "what is mortal is swallowed up by life" (2 Cor. 5:4), and further, "it is no longer I who live, but Christ who lives in me" (Gal. 2:20).[21]

Later in the same work, Nicholas compares our life as Christians to the grafting of a branch from one tree to the trunk of another: the characteristics of the branch are replaced by the characteristics of the new tree, and the fruit produced by the grafted branch are those of the new tree. So it is with ourselves as we are grafted onto Christ: now we live his life and produce his fruits. Such is the effect of the reception of the Holy Sacrament, of which we now plainly see the necessity (ibid.).

This necessity has been translated into practice by the authority of the Church. According to the Fourth Council of the Lateran (1215), all Christians, having come to the age of reason, must receive, at least at Easter, the sacrament of the Eucharist, after having confessed all of their sins (DS 812).

---

21. Nicholas Cabasilas, *The Life in Christ*, trans. Carmino J. de Catanzaro (Crestwood, N.Y.: St. Vladimir's Seminary Press, 1974), 115–16.

The precept holds only for those who have reached the use of reason. The Council of Trent "teaches that there exists no obligation for children who have not the use of reason to receive the sacramental communion of the Holy Eucharist: having been regenerated in the bath (Tit. 3:5) of baptism and incorporated into Christ, they cannot, at their age, lose the grace of children of God which they have received" (DS 1730, 1734).

The age of reason, whether for confession or for Communion, is the age at which the child begins to reason, that is, around seven years of age (DS 3530).

It is particularly important to recall the encouragement given by Pope Pius X to frequent, even daily, Communion. The Pope reacted against a mentality that tended to diminish the frequency of Communion in the name of a respect that kept the faithful at a distance from the Eucharistic Jesus by a sentiment of unworthiness. The consciousness of being sinners should surely lead persons to the sacrament of Penance, but after having received forgiveness the faithful have no reason to limit their recourse to Communion.

> The desire of Jesus Christ and of the Church that all of the faithful have daily access to the Sacred Supper has as its first objective that the faithful, joined to God through the sacrament, may there find strength to overcome their passions, purification from the slight faults that we commit every day and preservation from more grave sins to which human frailty is exposed. It is not primarily to secure honor and veneration for God, nor to have a recompense or reward for one's own virtues. Therefore the Sacred Council of Trent calls it an "antidote," thanks to which we are delivered from daily faults and preserved from mortal sins. (DS 3375)

Thus, it is decided that "frequent and daily Communion ought to be accessible to all of the faithful of whatever order or condition, in such a way that no one who is in the state of grace and approaches the sacred table with a right and devout intention should be denied access to it" (DS 3379).

Indeed, daily Communion was practiced in the primitive Church itself, since, according to the testimony of the Acts of the Apostles (2:46), every day in homes the breaking of the bread was practiced, a nourishment taken with that joy and simplicity of heart that are the characteristic marks of the Eucharistic meal. The first Christians had interpreted as referring to daily Communion Jesus' encouragement on the necessity of eating the flesh of the Son of Man and drinking his blood.

This daily recourse to Communion remains an ideal that should never be lost from view, even if concretely, for the great majority of Christians, the circumstances and conditions of life prevent its realization.

Sunday Communion, however, is more accessible. The precept obligating the faithful to attend at Sunday Mass implies an invitation to approach the Eucharistic table. Participation in the Eucharistic celebration cannot be complete if it does not conclude with Communion. The letter of the precept is discharged merely by attending Mass, but the Eucharist is fully shared only at the Eucharistic table.

Communion, Source of a Higher Energy

Meals secure for persons the strength of which they have need in order to live and act. In instituting the Eucharistic meal, Jesus has wished to place at the disposition of believers the necessary strength for the development of the entire Christian life.

Many have the experience of their own weakness, especially in the area of morality. Persons make serious resolutions, and then feel cheapened when they have not been able to keep them. The human will, even when firm and determined, can yield to its own frailty amid difficulties. The Gospel accounts have given us the example of Peter and the other Apostles, who had promised loyalty to the Master with a determination that they regarded as unshakable, and instead, at the moment of Jesus' arrest, all fled. Their good resolutions vanished just at the moment that they should have manifested themselves.

The only remedy for this frailty is divine assistance. Persons have need of a higher energy, which will enable them to overcome their weaknesses. Jesus wished to communicate this energy to us in a habitual manner through the Eucharist. And he communicates it not only with an extrinsic assistance, nor simply with an impulse that places the will in motion, but with a transformation of the whole person.

Indeed, with the Eucharist, Jesus becomes nourishment in such a way that his own energy passes to the person who feels weak. Unlike corporeal foods, which we assimilate and which become for us a supplier of life, the Eucharistic food assimilates us and transforms us, to introduce us to a higher life. Saint Augustine says to the Savior: "It is not you who will change me into yourself, as the food of your flesh, but you will be changed into me."[22] In the Eucharistic meal, Christ penetrates us with his assimilating power. It is he who transforms those who are nourished by his body. He communicates to them his divine energy.

Thus, the Eucharist responds to every situation of weakness. To those who complain of helplessness in the face of temptation, the Eucharistic meal offers the guarantee of a strength that was that of Jesus himself at the moment of confronting the temptations of his earthly life. To those who have received a mission and fear the obstacles arising in its fulfillment, the Eucharist secures the certitude of an unshakable perseverance in the realization of the task that they have received.

According to the recommendation of Pius X, already cited, Eucharistic Communion must be seen not as a reward for the pure and perfect, but as strength for the small and weak. The more believers discover their weakness, the more they are called to seek their spiritual strength in the Eucharist. The consciousness of having committed sins must never deter anyone from approaching the Eucharist, once forgiveness for one's failures has been sought. On the contrary, the conviction of personal frailty is an altogether ideal reason for placing one's hope in the strength that the Eucharistic Christ has willed to communicate to believers. In the Eucharist is revealed the great concrete principle that inspires the entire work of salvation, that is, the merciful goodness that stoops to the very weakest in order to lift them up. The strength of the meal is actually intended in a special way for those who recognize their frailty.

---

22. *Confessions*, book 1, chap. 7, no. 10.

The Eucharistic Meal, Source of Charity

The sign that, according to the intention of Christ, the Eucharist is a fount of charity is given in the fact that the moment chosen for the formulation of the new precept of love was the Last Supper. Jesus pronounced the commandment of mutual love on the occasion of the institution of a meal that also afforded the possibility of observing it. With the Eucharist, he rendered his disciples capable of loving one another as he had loved them.

Among the inner dispositions required for charity is the forgiveness of offenses. But on this point a difficulty could arise from the fact that a passage in the Gospels would seem to require it even before participation in the Eucharist: "When you are offering your gift at the altar, if you remember that your brother or sister has something against you, leave your gift before the altar and go; first be reconciled to your brother or sister, and then come and offer your gift" (Matt. 5:23–24).

We are dealing with an impressive warning concerning the attitude of charity required for the offerings of worship. In order to present one's offering, it is necessary to have made the effort of reconciliation and to have entered into heartfelt relations with one's erstwhile adversary. We cannot excuse ourselves from these efforts, not even with the excuse that the fault of the disagreement is the other's: indeed, according to Jesus' expression, it is not I who have something against my brother or sister, but my brother or sister who has something against me. Even in the instance in which the other were to be entirely at fault in the disagreement, it is I who must undertake a process of reconciliation. Only afterward may I present the offering.

Nevertheless, in concrete recommendations it is necessary always to underline the essential meaning of the lesson. Here the meaning is that an offering is deprived of value in God's eyes if it is presented by one who does not live in harmony with all, even with those who have done one some injury. The offering of those who have this will to harmony in their hearts will be pleasing to God. If they share in the Eucharist, they can ask of Christ, in Communion, the necessary strength of love, in order to live the desired reconciliation sincerely. Uniting their offerings to that of the Savior, they can expect from the Eucharist the grace of a total will to forgiveness and unity.

We can add that Jesus himself, at the Last Supper, limited himself to settling the dispute that had arisen among the Apostles for first place at table and, after having given an example of humble service with the washing of the feet, relied on the Eucharist to give the disciples, in the future, better dispositions for living in peace and harmony.

As a sacrificial meal, the Eucharist tends to communicate to the participants the love that has inspired the sacrifice, a love that spared nothing in order to secure the happiness of others and reached the pinnacle of heroism. The body and blood of Jesus, which are given as food and drink, contain all of the ardor of sacrifice.

Therefore the charity fostered and stimulated by the Eucharistic meal does not ignore the renunciations that the very teaching of Christ prescribes. It has not hesitated to ask sacrifices: "Do not resist an evildoer. But if anyone strikes you on the right cheek, turn the other also; and if anyone wants to sue you and take your coat, give your cloak as well; and if anyone forces you to go one mile, go also the second mile" (Matt. 5:39–42). The spontaneous reaction, which would consist in revolt against those who impose their will or do an injury, should be replaced with another reaction, which leaves room for generosity. But this can mean suffering. In this case, Christ does not speak of the Eucharist but wishes to contribute to the creation of an attitude of charity open to any eventuality and relies on the spiritual strength that will come from the Eucharist.

If with the Eucharist Jesus willed to give his disciples the strength to love one another as he had loved them, he gave them, with the gift of his body and blood, a power of love that knows no limits and that is efficacious in every human condition. He had no need of conveying with an enthusiastic hymn, as Paul has done, the unique excellence of charity, nor to say that charity "bears all things, believes all things, hopes all things, endures all things" (1 Cor. 13:7). Indeed, by way of indicating the model with the words "as I have loved you," he proposes his own life as that model — a true hymn to charity, besides being the source of all of the attitudes of love in human existence. Everything in his person is a revelation of love, and this person, in giving itself in the Eucharist, nourishes the human heart with love. It is impressive how John Chrysostom put his finger on the intimate link between the celebration of the Eucharist and the obligation of charity toward the very poorest. Indeed, according to Chrysostom, the sharing in the Lord's table brooks no inconsistencies here. "Let no Judas approach the table!" cries the homilist. And it is not a sufficient criterion of dignity to present oneself at the table with vessels of gold:

> Not of silver was that table, nor of gold the chalice from which Christ gave his disciples his blood.... Seek you to honor the body of Christ? Then permit him not to be naked, nor honor him here in the church with cloth of silk, thereupon to tolerate, away from here, that he die of cold and nakedness. The one who has said, "This is my body," has also said, "You have seen me hungry, and you have not fed me," and, "What you have not done for one of these least ones, you have not done for me." Then let us learn to be wise, and to honor Christ as he wills, disbursing your riches for the poor. God has need not of golden furniture, but of golden souls. What benefit is it if his table is covered with cups of gold, when he is dying of hunger? First satisfy him who hungers, and then, with what is left over, you shall adorn his table![23]

The Eucharistic Food, Wellspring of Joy

The first reference to the "breaking of the bread," that is, to the Eucharistic celebration, in the primitive Church indicated joy and simplicity of heart as distinctive marks of the meal (Acts 2:46).

Subsequently, in tradition, this joy that accompanies the Eucharist will frequently be recorded and stressed. Saint Thomas Aquinas features it in a particular manner: "The soul finds itself in

---

23. *Homily on the Gospel of Matthew,* 50, 2–4; PG 58:508–9.

spiritual delight. In a sense, it becomes inebriated with the divine goodness."[24]

A meal tends to produce euphoria. In selecting a meal as the sacramental sign of the gift of his own flesh and his own life, Jesus sought to place the emphasis in a special manner on the spiritual euphoria that was to constitute the climate of Christian life.

Not by chance did Jesus choose wine, so that we might better understand how the gift of his blood as drink is intended to produce a spiritual inebriation. The Eucharistic cup is an intoxicating one.

The miracle at Cana, with the transformation of water into wine, offers a first announcement, still very discreet, of the Eucharist. It gives us to understand in advance the abundance of joy that Jesus brings to humanity, besides the nature of that joy, which is that of a wedding banquet. We find the image of the banquet once more in the parable in which the Reign of God is compared to a feast that a king prepares for his son's wedding (Matt. 22:2). At the Last Supper, Jesus promises his disciples, "You may eat and drink at my table in my kingdom" (Luke 22:30).

The Eucharistic banquet is the image of the heavenly banquet, the banquet to which Jesus referred in proclaiming that he would return like the master of the house, at night, and that he would seat his slaves at table and begin to serve them (Luke 12:37). The heavenly banquet, then, has as its center Christ as bridegroom, as is also shown in the parable of the five wise virgins who enter with him into the banquet hall for the wedding (Matt. 25:1–13).

An anticipation of this banquet is offered us in the Eucharist. The Eucharistic repast is a meal that celebrates the covenant, a wedding banquet. It is connected with a sacrifice, whose recall could have been sorrowful, and which instead has the characteristic of changing sorrow into joy: "Your pain will turn into joy" (John 16:20).

Being the heavenly Christ in his state of glory, offering his body and blood in the Eucharist, he does so in order to pour forth his joy, giving himself as food and drink. The Son of Man, having "ascended to where he was before" (see John 6:62), cannot fail to

---

24. *Summa theologiae* 3, q. 79, aa. 1, 2.

be the source of a heavenly joy, which he seeks to pour forth on earth. The Eucharistic food never ceases to nurture gladness and to provoke the change from sorrow into joy that characterized the fulfillment of the redemptive drama.

Each Eucharistic celebration constitutes a new cause for joy for the Church and for humanity. Through joy, it fosters the authentic development of the work of evangelization, which proclaims the good news in a universe in which there abound such trials and sufferings of every sort. It is not a matter of a joy in which those who experience it close themselves up: on the contrary, they open themselves to all, so that these, too, may share a gladness superior to all others.

We are speaking, as well, of a joy that reveals the eschatological value of the Eucharistic meal. This joy presages the joy of heaven. It testifies to the ultimate intent of the Father, who has organized his entire design of salvation in order to secure the highest joy for humanity.

The Eucharist is a meal in which God is tasted, which gives the faithful to appreciate the savor of God and stimulates the desire to possess God. It contributes to the realization that no joy is comparable to the one that comes from on high: only the one who is fully happy can give the human heart to participate in this fullness of happiness. The Eucharist can offer only a token taste, but it does so by already giving Christ himself, in an invisible presence available to faith.

Eucharistic Meal, Upbuilding of the Body of Christ

Saint Paul, who makes use of the image of the body in order to present the Church as the body of Christ, had well understood the importance of the Eucharist in the formation of the life of that body: "Because there is one bread, we who are many are one body, for we all partake of the one bread" (1 Cor. 10:17).

The observation "Because there is one bread..." must be well understood in its context. Of itself, it could suggest that the Eucharistic meal is a simple consuming of the same bread and that the oneness of that bread is the foundation of the oneness of those who take part in the meal. But immediately preceding, Paul has demonstrated that the oneness is actually that of the body of Christ given as food. "The bread that we break, is it not a sharing in the body of Christ?" (1 Cor. 10:16). The cup is given to all: Communion is not realized first and foremost among those who drink of it, as a union primarily with one another, but rather, essentially, the Eucharist is Communion with the blood of Christ.

The blood of Christ, then, is a source of communion, as is the body of Christ. Then, commenting on the account of the institution, Paul speaks once more of those who eat the bread or drink the cup of the Lord, but adding that it is necessary to "discern the body" (see 1 Cor. 11:29), that is, to have a discernment of faith in order to become aware that in reality one is eating the body and drinking the blood of Christ in such a way as to be responsible to this body and this blood for the dispositions of soul with which one takes this meal, dispositions that could in given cases deserve a condemnation. Those who communicate in an unworthy way must "answer for the body and blood of the Lord" (see 1 Cor. 11:27).

This unworthy participation in the Eucharistic meal is of a grave nature, since it contradicts the essential finality of communion with the body and blood of Christ. It prevents the formation of one body among the participants. Communion tends precisely to form this unity: it tends to inaugurate a solid unity in the Christian community.

The aim for which the Eucharist has been instituted is precisely the formation and development of the one body called the Mystical Body of Christ. Those who share in the meal are engaged in the up-building of this Mystical Body: they are more profoundly inserted into it.

The first effect of the Eucharistic meal is a deeper union with Christ himself. It is an effect of communion in his body, his blood, his person. Then, inseparably, another effect is produced: that of a more profound connection with the entire community that lives the life of Christ, that is, with his Mystical Body, with the entire Church and each of its members.

This effect must be grasped in relation to the property of the Eucharistic repast as being a source of charity. The Eucharist stimulates the growth of the "whole body" in "building itself up in love" (Eph. 4:16). The Eucharist consolidates the connections of love that exist among all of the members of the body, through fidelity to the new commandment: "Love one another as I have loved you" (John 15:12; see 13:34). The Eucharist has the power to develop all of the aspects and all of the attitudes of reciprocal love, in such a way that from the head, who is Christ, the entire body "receives the strength to grow and build itself up in charity" (Eph. 4:16).

Conclusion

The Jubilee ought to have a hymn of praise to the Trinity for the gift of love revealed in the Incarnation of God. By way of a conclusion of this reflection on the mystery of the Eucharist, we recommend a hymn that we hope will help believers' faith to remain strong in the Eucharistic gift received. The object of the divine praise in the following hymn is the mystery of Eucharist itself, celebrated in the expression in which the poverty of human language falls least short of the glory of the divine: praise of God in song — that God who is rendered present and living in the sign of the consecrated bread and wine of the Eucharist.

> Zion, praise the Savior,
> praise your Guide and Shepherd
> in hymns and songs!
>
> Do your utmost,
> for he surpasses all praise,
> nor can you praise enough.
>
> Living, life-giving bread!
> The theme of your song today,
> The goal of your praise.
>
> At the table of the Holy Supper,
> He himself is given to the Twelve
> Truly and really.
>
> Let praises ring,
> Sing with joyful jubilation,
> Sing with all your spirit!
>
> For today is the festival
> of that sacred table,
> of its institution.

At this, the new King's table,
the new Passover of the New Law
ends the old condition.

The old age gives way to the new,
shadows are dispersed by truth
the night by light is scattered.

What Christ did at the meal,
this he required be done
in remembrance of him.

Taught by the sacred institution,
bread and wine we consecrate
to become salvation's host.

Christians have a dogma
that the bread becomes flesh,
the wine, blood.

What you fail to grasp or see,
a lively faith confirms,
beyond the order of natural things.

Both the different species —
signs alone, and not things —
conceal things of wonder.

Flesh is food, blood is drink:
still, the whole Christ abides
under either species.

Who receives does not sunder,
break or divide,
but receives the whole.

One takes or a thousand,
As much as they, so much the one,
nor is body or blood consumed away.

The good take, or the evil,
albeit to varied lot —
life, or demise.

Death to the evil, life to the good!
How different the outcome,
though the taking is the same!

Then, at the breaking of the sacrament,
be not affrighted, but recall,
each part or fragment
contains the whole.

The reality is not broken,
but only the sign,
nor is the state or stature
diminished of the signed.

Behold the bread of angels
become wayfarers' food!
Truly the bread of children,
not to be scattered to dogs.

Pretold in figures,
when Isaac is immolated,
when the Passover lamb is instituted,
when manna was given to our forebears.

Good Shepherd, true bread,
Jesus, show us mercy!
Feed us, guard us,
give us to see delights
in the land of the living.

Omniscient, omnipotent
nourisher of mortals here,
grant us places at your table there,
your co-heirs, and companions
of the holy citizens.
Amen. Alleluia!

crossroad